Living the Legacy of Adam

by Heidi Custin

Cover by Gary Powell

Cover Illustration by Gary Powell
Printed in the United States of America

ISBN – 978-1-0879-8519-0

Acknowledgments

Living the Legacy of Adam is dedicated to my daughter, Stephanie, and encourages me to explore the signs we are shown every day by our loved ones who have passed on to the heavenly realm. These signs might come in the form of dreams, the sending of animals, things or people our way, and other forms of visitations. She gives me peace in showing me that Adam still lives on in all of us. With great love, I also dedicate this book to my loving husband, Joe, who has stood by me through the good times and also through the pain and sorrow. He is the one who travels the state with me to advocate for others through the sharing of Adam's story. God put us together and together we will stay. I love you so very much!

Introduction

My daughter Stephanie is a gentle spirit who feels things deeply. She writes beautiful poetry and stories. Below, I share her story of Christmas Day 2015, the day our lives changed forever. In her story she uses the name Abel in place of Adam. I remember Adam saying when he was doing well that one day he would have a son and name him Abel. I am not sure if this is why she chose Abel or if it somehow softens the blow in telling her story.

Christmas Day 2015
by Stephanie Custin

I glance at the clock on my wall. It's 11:50 a.m. Wow, I think to myself. I can't believe it's almost noon already. I am completely alone in my apartment, sitting on my couch with the TV on mute. A quiet atmosphere makes it easy for me to become lost in my thoughts. This is the first time in my entire life that I have been alone on Christmas morning. Part of me feels a little saddened by this, but the other part of me is fine with it. Solitude means relief. I think about everything I have been through in my life.

My journey on this earth hasn't been easy, but it has brought me a lot of wisdom. I believe that everything happens for a reason, even the bad things. However, never in a million years would I have guessed that I would be the victim of a violent domestic relationship. For over six years, I tolerated abusive behavior, and for the most part of that relationship, I knew in my heart that he wasn't the one I was supposed to end up with, but I had never had the courage to leave him.

Or so I thought. Even though being with him wasn't my destiny, it was part of my journey. Unbeknown to him, the day arrived when fate came knocking at my door and swept me off my feet. The day that fate found me was the day I changed. I immediately became callous towards him and decided to end the relationship. During that transition period, I was given many opportunities to get revenge, but I had decided that walking away from him and leaving him to cry over me was punishment enough.

I abruptly snap out of my thoughts. I get up from the couch and make my way into the kitchen to get something to drink. As I open the refrigerator door, my mind starts to drift again...

It's funny how things happen in life. Little did I know, that being with the wrong person for so long was putting me on the right path to finding the right person. The new man in my life is the one I refer to as "Fate" because the day we met each other for the first time, we both knew that it was fate that brought us together. It was at that point that everything in my life had started to make sense, as if he was the missing puzzle piece. I knew that every situation in my life had been timed correctly, so that I would be in the right place at the right time, for the sole purpose of meeting him. Thinking about him gives me a warm feeling. I had almost forgotten what that was like.

As I take a sip of my water, I can hear my phone ringing from the other room. I rush over to answer it and notice it's my mom. "Hey, Mom," I say, greeting her.

"Hey, Stephie! We are about 15 minutes away from your apartment," she says in a sweet tone.

"Okay, sounds good. I'll be waiting for you outside," I say.

My parents were visiting family about two hours away. My

brother and I had opted out of that holiday trip. We had stopped go-ing with our parents to celebrate Christmas with extended family years ago. Since my brother still lived with my parents, my parents had in-formed me about a week prior that they planned on picking me up from my apartment on their way back into town. Then the four of us would spend Christmas together as a family, at their house. I hang up the phone with my mom, then swiftly get myself together and make my way outside.

When I exit my apartment building, I am immediately sur-rounded by the frigid winter air. I sit down on the steps at the entrance and bring my arms closer to my body in an attempt to keep myself warm. BRRR! It's freezing outside! I wonder if I have enough time to run inside to grab a warmer jacket and maybe some gloves, too.

In the middle of debating what to do, I am suddenly consumed by an ominous feeling. This is odd, I think. Something doesn't feel right. I am instantly on guard and checking my surroundings. It doesn't last long because my focus quickly becomes averted when I see my parents pulling up. In anticipation of relief from the cold winter air, I jog towards their car, then jump inside in a hurry. "Hey," I say pleasant-ly while rubbing my hands together to keep them warm.

"Hey! It's my favorite daughter!" my dad exclaims.

"I'm your only daughter, Dad," I say with a wry grin. My dad exits my apartment complex's parking lot and turns onto the main road. I sit quietly in the back seat, staring out the window. For some reason I start to feel that same ominous feeling again. I'm not sure where it is coming from, but something doesn't feel right.

"So how was your trip?" I ask, breaking the silence.

"It was great!" my mom answers. "Everyone asked about you. They all miss you a lot."

"I miss them, too," I lie. "Maybe I can go with you next Christmas so I can see everyone," I lie again. I have never been too keen on seeing extended family for the holidays, and my parents know that, but they always accept the "maybe next time" false hope I continuously give them. I quickly change the subject by asking about my brother. "Have you talked to Abel?"

"No, I haven't," my mom replies. "But before we left, he did mention that he was having problems with his phone charging properly."

I know my brother's phone is off because I had tried calling him earlier that morning, but I wanted to ask them anyway. About ten minutes later, we arrive at their house. My parents begin grabbing their luggage out of the car as I make my way towards the front door. I am filled with immense anticipation to see my brother, as always. We are only a year and a half apart, and we have always been close.

I twist the doorknob and make a dramatic entrance by yelling his name in an obnoxious, silly way. I am not sure why, but that is something I have done since childhood.

Well, this is odd. The house is completely silent. I shout his name again, but this time a little louder. "ABEL!" Still no answer. "Abel?" Silence. I go into his bedroom. He is not in there. My parents start making their way into the house with their luggage. "Mom, did Abel leave or something?" I ask.

"I don't think he would leave, honey. He knew about our Christmas plans," my mom informs me.

"Well, where is he then?" I ask. "I've been calling his name. He's not answering and he's not in his room."

"Is he on the deck smoking a cigarette?" my mom asks me.

"No," I reply.

"Is he in the bathroom?"

"No."

"Is he in the garage?"

"No." I decide to check his room again. Maybe he's in his bed, sleeping underneath his blanket. Maybe I just overlooked him or something.

I stand in the doorway of his room, scanning it more carefully this time. He is definitely not in there. But where can he be? My parents, now very alarmed at his absence, start calling his name.

I am still standing in the doorway of his empty bedroom, and when I glance behind me, I notice that my parents have decided to check the basement. I hear them opening the door, followed by the sound of their feet thumping down the wooden steps. Nothing can prepare me for what comes next.

The sound I hear is so haunting that it causes me to instantly freeze up. It is my mother. She is screaming the most unbearable, agonizing scream that I have ever heard in my entire life. I know that something horrible has happened.

I sprint through the living room towards the basement. When I approach the top of the basement staircase, I don't hesitate, quickly rushing down the steps. As soon as I make it to the bottom, I see something that stops me in my tracks. "OH! MY! GOD!" I scream. I can see my brother clearly. His body is dangling from a rope that has been tied around his neck. A knocked-over chair lies nearby. My heart instantly drops to my stomach. This can't be happening, I think desperately; this can't be happening. This isn't real; this isn't real. He can't be dead. Please tell me he's not dead.

My mom is frantic, and she runs up the stairs, rushing past me. As she dials 911, she is screaming, "OH GOD! OH GOD!"

I just collapse there, frozen on the stairs. The horrifying sight that is in front of me has left me in complete disbelief. My dad is standing underneath my brother with his arms wrapped around his legs, desperately trying to keep the pressure off his neck by hoisting him upwards. I cannot believe this. This must be a dream. This cannot be real.

I use both of my hands to cover my ears while squeezing my eyes shut. All I can hear is the sound of my own voice inside of my head. "WAKE UP! THIS ISN'T REAL! WHAT'S TAKING YOU SO LONG? WAKE UP NOW!" I can't breathe. I NEED TO GET OUT OF HERE NOW! I stand up from the staircase, and after taking two steps, my legs suddenly cannot hold me up, and I collapse again. What is happening to me? My mind is moving fast, but my body is moving so slowly. Is this what being in shock feels like? The only thing I can do at this point is to start crawling up the stairs on my hands and knees, and I don't look back. Not even once.

When I finally make it to the top of the staircase, I see my mother in the living room. She is sitting on the couch, talking to the 911 operator. She has tears of grief and pain pouring down her cheeks. Seeing my mother in such despair gives me an unimaginable feeling of sadness. My heart explodes with unbearable heartache, and I realize that this moment will change all of us forever. My parents and I will never be the same.

Struggling, I stand up from the staircase and stumble towards the front door. My mind is battling itself with nonstop waves of disbelief that keep hitting me hard. I wish I could run from this feeling. I wish I could just wake up and this would all be over. When I finally make it outside, I run to the side of the house and fall to my knees. I am unbothered by the winter air and embrace the piercingly cold wind coming at me. My vision then becomes completely obscured by tears.

I feel like I am trapped in a permanent nightmare. All I want to do is escape this moment. All I want is some relief. As I sit there sobbing on the ground, I notice police cars and an ambulance arriving. I remain sitting on the side of the house. I don't feel like talking to anybody. I just want to be alone.

A few moments later, I am approached by two officers. "Hey sweetheart, your mother is looking for you," one of them says to me.

I look up at him with red cheeks and makeup smeared under my eyes. Then I hesitantly ask, "Is he...is he dead?" I can tell he hears the agony in my voice. I can tell he doesn't want to tell me the truth.

The officer looks down at the ground, and then he softly says, "Yes."

They both suddenly became a huge blur as my eyes fill up with tears again. "No! No! No!" I expel the words at them as if it is their fault that this is happening.

"Come on, let's go inside," one of them suggests.

"I don't want to!" I shout.

"How about you try to see if you can stand up, and if you need help walking, you can lean on us," the officer says patiently.

"But I don't know if I can go back in there," I say.

"I think your mother wants you in there with her," he replies.

I hesitate for a moment and start thinking about my poor mother and what she must be feeling. "Alright," I finally agree. I now have an officer on each side of me, and they lift me off the ground with such ease that I feel as light as a feather. We then proceed to walk towards the house. I am still having trouble processing everything that is happening, and I start to feel weak and dizzy. I am crying even harder now, and walking starts to become difficult. I start dragging my feet.

Both officers are so patient and kind to me, and when they notice me struggling, they both offer me support, and we slowly make our way back to the house.

After they take my brother's body out of the house, my mother starts contacting friends and family to give everyone the bad news. The next several hours consist of multiple people showing up at their house to show their support. Even though I appreciate everyone's effort, I still have a strong urge to distance myself. I know this is just the beginning. I know the rest of my life will be spent healing and wishing this day had never even existed.

Chapter 1
Recap of Adam's Life

As Told to First Responders during Crisis Intervention Training

My name is Heidi Custin, and I am here to tell you about our family and living with mental illness. I bring pictures to validate that we are a family, just like many of you who have real people in these stories. Sometimes it is more believable when you see something tangible. You will see pictures of all stages of life to get an idea of how a "normal" family transforms into something we never saw coming. Thank you all for all that you do. We support you. We appreciate you taking time out of your busy lives to learn about how to handle a crisis situation with someone living with mental illness. We know that your job is tough enough without having to sort through a situation in an instant and make a decision about whom you are dealing with.

We were a family like any other. My husband Joe and I have been married for over thirty years, which statistically in our world is rare! Joe is my rock, and I am blessed to have him in my life. We are always there for one another. Thirty-plus years ago, we had it in our heads that life was going to be great. We were going to have children and they would be happy because we would do all the "right" things that make up a happy family! You never in your wildest dreams believe anything horrible could happen to that adorable, sweet baby when you hold him or her in your arms for the first time.

We had two children, Stephanie and Adam, born seventeen months apart. We took them to church on Sundays and enrolled them in religious education. Joe was Adam's Boy Scout leader. I was the leader of Stephanie's Girl Scout troop. Joe helped coach all the sports teams our children participated in. We ate dinner together every night. We raised them in a nice neighborhood full of great families and influences. Because these are all the things you do to raise happy, healthy, smart kids, who will in turn contribute greatly to society one day, right? Both kids were active, playful, funny, well-adjusted children and had many great friends. They lacked for nothing. They had two college-educated parents working in professional jobs. They were loved and they knew it! We spent time together both at home and traveling.

When Stephanie was six, she had a nearly fatal tick bite. Doctors believed that this bite contributed to her pancreas ceasing to function, and by the age of ten, she was a type 1 Diabetic on insulin for the rest of her life. She was often sick, and our focus shifted from Adam to her much of the time.

Imagine our shock when at the age of fourteen, Adam made his first suicide attempt! Were we not paying enough attention to him? The psychiatrist diagnosed Adam with clinical depression. As time went on, we were unsure if this was what we were actually seeing. He started hanging out with a different set of friends, wore dark clothes, smoked cigarettes and pot, drank alcohol, and progressed into harder drugs. He hallucinated and ranted and raved, seeing and hearing things that we didn't.

When Adam was around the age of sixteen, I asked his doctor if it could be Schizophrenia he was suffering from. The doctor wasn't ready to label a young teen with that. Or could it be the drugs? Was he just a bad kid acting out? How could we know? We knew nothing about mental illness or how teenagers behaved until our children became them.

From age fourteen to twenty-one, Adam made at least one or two suicide attempts every year. Many people thought he was looking for attention, but these were major attempts, from trying to commit "suicide by police officer" with a gun, throwing himself in front of a car in fast traffic, and many attempts by overdoses that doctors said were big enough to kill a horse. He was 5'6" tall and around 130 pounds in his teens.

Stephanie began cutting herself around the age of fifteen, so Joe and I really had our hands full. She was a bit more manageable, as she didn't have what we came to know later as psychotic episodes.

When Joe received a promotion with State Farm Insurance, we moved from Broken Arrow, Oklahoma, after twenty years of living there. Stephanie and Adam moved with us at nineteen and eighteen years of age. In 2011, when Adam was twenty, I came across a pamphlet I must have picked up in Oklahoma somewhere. Adam was in and out of psychiatric hospitals and doctors' offices so many times, who knows where I got it? It said NAMI, National Alliance on Mental Illness, on it. We were at our wits' end with frustration over the "behavior" of our son, the sleepless nights, and the costly hospital bills. Kansas City had a NAMI chapter, so I made the call.

Joe and I took the Family to Family class, and it changed everything. Most of all, it taught us how to more effectively communicate with our son. During one class, we scanned the column of symptoms of Paranoid Schizophrenia, and both of us checked off all of the boxes! At least we now knew what we were dealing with, but we were frightened out of our minds.

During the summer of 2012, we moved into a new house. Steph and her boyfriend moved into an apartment. For the first month Adam lived with Stephanie, until he became too much for her to handle. Then it was just Joe, Adam, and I. Quickly, we both took training to be support group facilitators, and Joe became certified to teach Family to Family classes. Adam could see our desire to help him and soon opened up to his doctors and received the diagnosis we were expecting: Paranoid Schizophrenia. In early November 2012, for the first time ever, Adam requested to go to Research Psychiatric Hospital.

However, then he met a young lady who, knowing his self-destructive intent and wanting to help him achieve it, supplied him with 100 morphine pills. One Sunday night he placed them all in the shape of a heart and took a picture of them with his phone. He swallowed pill after pill until only three remained on his pillow. That evening Joe went into Adam's room to say good night and found him slumped over his laptop on the floor between his bed and the wall. He asked him if he was okay. Adam said he was tired, and Joe helped him into his bed. Adam said, "I love you, Dad." This was very rare in our world.

The next day, Monday, happened to be a long workday for both of us, and we worked long into the evening. When we finally got home, we each looked in on Adam, and he appeared to be sleeping. We were relieved because he had been ranting for days, and we were happy to get two nights of sleep in!

On Tuesday, I was at work in Shawnee, Kansas, a forty-minute drive from home, when I received a frantic call from Joe. I couldn't understand a word he said, he was crying so hard. "Is he gone?" I asked. He didn't know. They were loading him into an ambulance as we spoke. I raced to St. Joseph Hospital. There, we were given the worst news possible. Adam's organs were shutting down, and he had no brainwave activity. He was going to die. We had to take him off of life support. After four days and nights waiting by his bedside for him to die, he suddenly woke up!

Impossible, they said, but it happened. He was still as psychotic as ever, and no rehabilitation center would take him until he got the psychological issues under control. That is the worst case of stigma! He'd had a stroke and couldn't walk right, among other issues.

A couple of weeks later, Research Psychiatric Hospital took him in. In the space of only two weeks, Adam went from walking with a cane, to using a walker, to sitting in a wheelchair, to having his head supported by a wheelchair strap. Then we found him in his bed soaked in urine and unresponsive once again. At that point, the brain unit at Research took charge of him. Five-and-a-half weeks later, he woke up again! Only he weighed a mere 97 pounds, ate through a feeding tube, and couldn't move or speak above a whisper.

Finally, Meadowbrook Rehabilitation accepted him. Adam had to relearn everything we take for granted, like eating, talking, walking, reading, and writing! Everything. But he heard no voices! Adam returned to us this wonderful young man, the man we always knew was trapped inside his mind. He became active in NAMI, in a program called In Our Own Voice, telling his story to others who lived with mental illness, encouraging them to get the help that they needed.

In May 2015, he was accepted into Longview College to become a social worker and help others who were like him. He was supposed to start in August. We took a family trip to Montana with my sister Ann and her boys. During that trip, it seemed that Adam's brain found new pathways, and the Schizophrenia returned. He had vowed before that if this ever happened again to him, he would take his meds, see his doctors, and not self-medicate. He followed through with this promise, but nothing he did would help his symptoms.

Adam ended his life on Christmas Day 2015, at the age of twenty-four. Because Adam had retained all his short- and long-term memories, we were able to learn so much about people who live with Schizophrenia. He was our miracle. He talked about how much he always loved us but couldn't communicate it to us through the walls that his illness put up. One time he found a journal he had written in at the age of ten. In one paragraph it said, "We just got our first dog today. In order to get rid of the voices, I have to die."

I told him he couldn't have been sick at ten. He said, "Ah, Mom. Don't you understand? I heard voices at two and thought everyone did; only no one else ever talked about it, so I didn't either." This at least was a relief for us because we know knew he didn't cause the illness with drugs.

So, you see, we are a family like anyone else. We love fiercely and fight for our children, no matter whether they have cancer, diabetes, or mental illness. Thank you again for your time. Joe also shares stories about our own encounters with police and having them in our home during crises. Certainly not how we expected our life with kids to go! We talk about the National Alliance on Mental Illness. We lead them into a question-and-answer session. Tears often flow throughout the room, and that's okay. We know we might have changed someone's mind. Questions and engaging follow.

We have been giving Crisis Intervention Training speeches since 2013. It was important when Adam was living and even more so now. We can't bear the thought of another family losing a member to suicide because of the fear of coming out with a mental illness and actually receiving help. This is our life now. Advocating and putting our superhero masks on to save lives. Except we are not superheroes. We are two very sad, lost souls who are fighting for our own sanity as much as anyone else's.

Chapter 2
Suicide

Suicide. We have all heard the word or associated it with someone else we have known. I remember when my friend Steve died by suicide as a teen, and asking "Why? What could have gone wrong? Why would anyone do something like that?" I pondered it periodically over the years, but I eventually moved on and "got over" it. I think about his parents now, whom I never knew, and I realize they must have never gotten over it. When it happens directly to you, you never do. I felt Steve didn't show any signs because he seemed happy and joked around. He didn't appear to be depressed. I can look back now and see the signs he left for us. He gave personal things away. He went around wishing people well in life. It seemed strange at the time, but he was saying his last good-byes.

In college, when a student named Barbara told me about her brother's suicide, I sympathized with her but couldn't empathize because I hadn't gone through it as closely as she did. I wish I would have had her talk more about it then, because now I know she needed to. I simply couldn't wrap my brain around why anyone would do this, and the mere thought of it frightened me.

It still does. But this...this was our son—our only son. He. Died. By. Suicide. He was dead! Adam was really dead! No miracles could save him now. He was gone forever! Or was he? Where was he? "Where ARE you, ADAM?" both Joe and I would scream many times over. We had to plan a service for our son, a "Celebration of Life". What? Celebrate? NO! We can't have a Celebration of Life, I thought.

He can't be dead! He is only twenty-four! "God, this is a mistake!" I cried. "You returned him before. Please bring him back again! We will do anything you ask of us! Take me! Just not our boy!" We were already working on the five stages of grief: Denial, Anger, Bargaining, Depression, and Acceptance. I had studied these in college. Now I was living them, and not necessarily in the right order. Sometimes I experienced them all at once, but never the last one! NO, I thought, that isn't happening and won't ever happen!

Signs of suicide. We knew the signs, yet still didn't see them or denied what was happening right in front of us. We could excuse ourselves for our own faults and wrongdoings for what we didn't know about mental illness (until we did know, and then accountability had to be taken). But suicide? We had learned not only through NAMI what those signs were, but our son had made several attempts on his life. So why didn't we see it?

Maybe what threw us off was that he'd never really shown those signs before. He'd always been so drugged up and out of it, so psychotic, that it must not have been important to him to say goodbye or give things away. At this time in his life, even in the midst of psychosis, he was loving, kind, and somewhat present with us. He did give things away. He gave me his razor that he treasured and for which he had shipments of blades delivered monthly. He took me shopping. He bought us all things. I mistook it all for Christmas generosity and hoped it was a sign he was feeling better.

I was wrong. Dead wrong, and that is something I will probably feel guilty for the rest of my life. Below are some signs of suicide. If someone you know has been showing these signs lately, I implore you to take it very seriously!

Warning Signs of Suicide:

Talk

If a person talks about:

- Being a burden to others
- Feeling trapped
- Experiencing unbearable pain
- Having no reason to live
- Killing themselves

Mood

People who are considering suicide often display one or more of the following moods:

- Depression
- Loss of interest
- Rage
- Irritability
- Humiliation
- Anxiety

Behavior

Specific things to look out for include:

- Increased use of alcohol or drugs
- Looking for a way to kill themselves, such as searching online for means or materials
- Acting recklessly
- Withdrawing from activities
- Isolating from family and friends
- Sleeping too much or too little

- Visiting people or calling to say good-bye
- Giving away prized possessions
- Aggression

Adam exhibited most of these warning signs for a few months before he completed his suicide. I am pretty sure that he had it all planned out and knew he had the window of opportunity the night we were to be gone. He also was very pleasant the day we went shopping. It is clear to me that he had made a decision that he was satisfied with. He felt he would be free from all the pain soon.

Chapter 3
Nightmares and Dreams

From the first night after Adam took his life, I would dream of his footsteps coming up the stairs, coming closer and closer and then into our room. Then I would awaken suddenly to look for him and see him swinging out from the wall beside me, hanging from a noose. Joe said, "You can't un-see it." He was so right, but was this the image I would have of him for the rest of my life? Hanging? Lifeless?

Fortunately, the hanging images didn't last beyond the first year. But I would have other nightmares, usually ones that resulted in Adam saving me or our family. Some of them were bizarre! One night I dreamt that Joe and I were traveling by car somewhere in the United States with our children. They were around ten and eleven years old. A car full of dangerous-looking men pulled up alongside us at a stoplight going through a town. They stared at us and began laughing.

I told Joe I felt uncomfortable, and he said to not look at them. We stopped to eat at a nice restaurant with a long oval-shaped sidewalk that wound around to its parking lot. There was a long awning over the door that led down the sidewalk a ways, and it really darkened the path at night. When we left, we came out from under the awning, and Joe said he would get the car and pull it around to pick us up. He ran off ahead, and the kids and I slowly walked in his direction. We were spread out. Suddenly, a car full of scary-looking men come racing into the lot. They were coming straight towards us with semi-automatic guns shooting out the windows. We were running and screaming. Joe was in our car, yelling for us to hurry.

Suddenly, I heard a voice yelling from off in the distance, in the opposite direction, "Run!" I turned to look who had yelled this, and it was Adam. He was twenty-four again. He was smiling at us, glowing, his arms outstretched while the bullets came his way. Bullets were fired at him repeatedly but never took him down or harmed him in any way. Stephanie and I got into the car and Joe drove off. Adam had been watching out for us, keeping us safe.

I had other dreams in which the children were at a young age, where he would suddenly appear and save us from threats. He would be grown and Stephanie would be little. I couldn't understand what that was about.

In one such dream, Joe and I were traveling through a tunnel on our motorcycle. Three-year-old Stephanie was trying frantically to keep up with us on her tricycle. She was clearly in danger of getting run over or crashing. Suddenly, adult Adam stepped in, almost floating in the air, and carried her and the trike to safety. I had many dreams like these, of him saving us.

Stephanie, on the other hand, had nightmares that were horrific. She dreamt about Adam killing himself over and over in various manners. One such dream she related to me took place in Oklahoma. In it, we were living in our first house, and Adam ran into the street in front of a car and was mangled. She witnessed it. She ran into the house screaming, looking for me, yelling for her mama, and she couldn't find me. The nightmare was especially upsetting to me, thinking about how traumatic this was for my girl, how alone she must have felt without her brother, her sidekick in life. In her dreams, he was leaving her over and over in various ways, leaving her with no one to turn to—no mother to be found to save him from death or her from trauma.

I know Joe has had his share of nightmares, too. He wouldn't relate them too much, but he would writhe around in his sleep, tossing fitfully and screaming or crying out. No, you can't un-see what happened.

As time passed during the last three years since Adam's death, the nightmares became less frequent, and dreams of beauty began to replace them. Every now and then a nightmare still appears, but mostly I have good dreams. One such good dream I had depicted Adam as a toddler. We were in a large room full of extended family. Everyone was passing Adam around the room. His arms were outstretched towards me, and he cried the entire time, "Mama, Mama!" It wasn't until he was in my arms that the crying ceased. He looked up at me with huge blue eyes as if to say, "This is where I belong."

In real life, as Adam grew up with mental illness, people told us that we must have been the cause of it; that we were poor parents, and other similar hurtful statements. It was the easiest thing to say out of frustration because others couldn't fix Adam's problems any better than we could. So to them, somehow, we must have been at fault. We lived far away from these people, so I am not sure how they knew what we did or didn't do, but that is all resolved today. The point is that my subconscious mind still harbored those feelings of not being a good mother to my children. Maybe somehow I caused him to leave this world by suicide. So, in this particular dream, I believe Adam was trying to tell me that he felt safest with me; that it wasn't my fault. That he knew he was loved and wanted.

If you are going through the loss of a suicide, you understand the enormous amount of guilt that follows, even if it is not deserved. My mother passed away in 2018. A few weeks prior, I'd had a dream about this motel in Belton, Missouri, where homeless people live. Our church brings them food and any other items they might need. I have never been there, but I dreamt I was there feeding people with Joe, and he said, "Hey, should we visit your mother while we are here?" My mother had been placed in a nursing home in Columbia, Missouri, the week following Adam's Celebration of Life. She lay in bed twenty-four hours a day.

Yet, in the dream, I said, "Sure, let's go visit her."

We went to her house and knocked on her door. She answered, using a cane for support. She told us that our kids were visiting and said what a coincidence that we showed up on the same day.

I said, "You mean Stephanie? Because Adam died, you know?" (This was actually something that came up during every visit with her. She would ask me if Adam had died. I would tell her that he had, and she would tell me how sad that was, then go on to another subject.)

"No," she said, "both of them are here." I looked beyond her, and there they both were! "Adam, I can't believe you are here!" I cried. "You died!"

He smiled his glorious smile and responded, "Mom, I am always with her, just as I am with you, Dad, and Stephanie. I will be here to greet her when she comes home."

Shortly after this dream, Mom passed away. Was Adam sending me a message through my dreams? I hope so. Dreams like these give me peace and help get me through it all. Following her death, I had another dream of Mom and Adam together on a lake, in a boat. My mom grew up on Lake Erie. She spent her childhood swimming, boating (she owned her own boat), and ice skating on that lake. Adam and Mom appeared to be about the same age—late twenties, early thirties—in swimsuits, looking beautiful and full of life. I took it as a sign that he is with her and that they are both free of the demons that tortured them here on earth.

Recently, I had a nightmare about my father. I was standing on one side of a long counter, and he was glaring at me. He looked to be around sixty. He looked as if he was going to harm me and reached over the counter with a gnarly hand to grab me. I yelled at him, "No more! You cannot hurt me anymore!" and woke up.

A few days later, I dreamt of Papa again, along with the entire family…and I mean entire! All the relatives, long or recently passed. Grandparents, great aunts and uncles, my beloved Aunt Jane and Uncle Don, Mom, and Adam and some I never knew. Joining them were all the living members, too. It was a big family reunion the likes of which we'd had so many of in years past. Many times we would congregate in cabins near a river, but in this dream, they were in an enormous cabin. It was so large, it seemed to go on for miles and miles with several stories (I imagined this was our family mansion in heaven). It was elaborately built in rustic fashion. All those who passed were young, around thirty years of age, socializing, happy, and glowing. The living appeared to be their correct age.

I arrived late to the party. I had gotten lost on curvy, seemingly unending roads. I have always said I have direction dyslexia, and I know there is a name for what I have. It flips directions in my brain somehow and can be scary at times. Thank God for GPS! I love it, but wherever we were, it was not working! Finally, I found my way there. With a bit of trepidation on encountering my father, I approached the cabin. When I was a child, my lack of direction had frustrated him. He could find his way around the world. Why couldn't this child find her way around in small town America? He told me I was stupid.

Well, in this dream when I met up with him, I said, "I am sorry I am late, Papa. But, you know me. Always lost and confused. I am not your brightest child."

With great love in his eyes and kindness in his tone, Papa quickly corrected me. "Heidi, that is not true! You are very smart! Don't let anyone tell you differently, ever again!" Through that dream, I made peace with my father.

In my previous book, *Adam's Contract With God*, I mentioned the babies I had lost and how Adam told me that two were boys and one was a girl, when I had believed they were all girls. One night, I dreamt of all my children, including my living child, Stephanie. Stephanie and I were standing together across from the other four, who were in a line as if Adam was going to introduce them to us. Strange thing is, I knew them by sight! All of them (once again) appeared to be around thirty years old. My oldest is Stephanie, and she is in her early thirties. She is around 5'5" and has large, olive green eyes, and long, straight, light honey brown hair. The next one would have been Stephen. He was tall, around 6'3", slender like Adam, with dark brown, wavy hair like Adam's, only darker. His eyes were even darker blue than Adam's. Then there was my middle child, Adam himself. Adam stood about 5'6", with wavy brown hair and bright blue eyes. Next to Adam was Lewis. He was around Adam's height and was slim, with straight, blond hair, much like Joe's was when he was younger. He had lighter blue eyes like his dad. The youngest was my baby, Amy. She looked to be about ninety-five pounds and had straight, long blond hair and light green eyes. So my boys had blue eyes and my girls had green! Wow! I could see both Joe and me in all of them! They all just smiled and looked beautiful and glowing.

When I told Stephanie about the dream, she was astounded and told me that the girl I had described was always with her. She saw her spirit all the time but had never known who she was. She told me that it made total sense now.

I think that maybe nightmares and dreams heal us on our journey. In our nightmares, we confront what frightens us, yet we are braver and stronger than in waking life. Our good dreams show us how far we have come on our journey. They give us the peace we need, especially when loved ones pass away. They show us the truth and beauty of what is and what awaits us when we, too, pass away. No fear, no pain. Just love and forgiveness. Stephanie told me a few months ago that she feels that Adam has a child out there somewhere. A grandchild, wow. Someone who possibly looks like Adam. That would be nice, I thought.

My mind wandered to when it might have happened, how old the child would be. Was it when he was a teenager living in Oklahoma? That is what I guessed. The child could be twelve years old! Strangely enough, I had a dream just last night. A lady contacted me and said she wanted to tell me something about Adam and that it was important. She had read *Adam's Contract With God* and didn't know until she read the book that he had been ill or that he had died. I agreed to meet her at her house. It was in Kansas City. A lady met me at the door. She said she was the woman's assistant and that the woman had gone to pick up a child at school. She welcomed me into the room.

There were a few children in there. It thought it was perhaps a daycare. I saw a baby with beautiful blue eyes and commented on them. She said, "Wait until you see Addie." She opened up a photo album, and the first thing I saw was a picture of a baby with my eyes, Adam's eyes. She looked like we both did as babies. Then there were more pictures of the same child until the age of four.

The woman who contacted me walked in at that moment. She was about my age and had the little girl with her, a girl version of Adam at four. Or me. Blond hair like we both had and those same blue eyes. "This is Addie," she said. "Short for Adelaide. (Interestingly enough, that is another version of my name, Heidi.) "My daughter named him after Adam. She was obsessed with him, but sadly he didn't return her feelings. She never told him that she was pregnant."

I thought back to a situation that happened in real life outside of my dream, but remembered it in the dream, too: there was a girl whom Adam dated briefly. We never met her but would see him talking to her near her car parked out in front of our house. She was the mother of this child in my dream. Her mother told me she had "problems". This child was Adam's. The girl had become pregnant before Adam got sick again, that same year. The baby had been born in December, the month he died. The grandmother was raising her as her own, and when she found out about us, she wanted us to know her and be a part of her life, too. In my dream I was overjoyed.

When I woke up, I was disappointed. At the same time, I couldn't help but wonder after what Stephanie had told me, What if? That may not happen in my world, but I can still dream.

A few nights before, I had a dream that our family was vacationing in a foreign land. We rented a two-story house near the ocean. Between the back of the house and the ocean was a huge concrete square built into the ground that narrowed like a cone as it went down. A square cone. Funny dream thought. It was used to catch water and drain in if the tide came up too high so it wouldn't reach the house. It was full of water most of the time. Our kids appeared to be around nineteen and eighteen years of age. It was apparent in the dream that we were aware of Adam's illness and concerned about him the entire trip, as we would be in real life. (In real life we had taken a cruise with family and friends in a foreign place, and Adam would lay on the beach all day, sneaking alcohol when someone would sell it to him.) In my dream, he disappeared and we feared the worst, that he had taken his life. I was worried he would be found in the concrete square when the water drained. The authorities were contacted, and the island was thoroughly searched. No one found him. Would he wash up on the beach one day?

The dream seemingly lasted for months as we decided we would not return to the States until he was found, dead or alive. One day I found his wallet sitting on a window sill next to his dad's and mentioned it to Joe. He said that Adam had left it behind with money and his driver's license, everything still inside it. Shortly after that, I looked out at the ocean, and there on the sand lay Adam, between the shore and the square. I thought he was dead. Then Joe ran out the back door from the lower level and called out to him. He sat up! He said, "Hey Dad! Did you know there are cool places here like rehab for people with mental illnesses? They take good care of you and help you get better. I checked in to one. I'm sorry I worried you, but I was really sick. But now I am doing well!" He looked so happy. We felt happy, too.

I then woke up feeling very disoriented. My entire body was in pain. I got up to use the bathroom and felt dizzy and fell into the wall to steady myself. It took a while to realize that it was only a dream, and I broke down crying.

Joe asked me if I was okay, and I said, "Oh you know, one of those Mommy moments." I never have to explain myself to him because he gets those moments, too. Moments that sometimes come out of nowhere and hit me like the first day we knew Adam was gone. It took me a about an hour to be able to speak about the dream, but when I did, it occurred to me it was another message assuring us that he was doing well. "I was really sick, but now I am well." It reminded me of the line from the hymn, "Amazing Grace": "I once was lost, but now I am found." Maybe I had that dream because we are heading into September, the month for suicide awareness, then into the holidays, which are tough for us.

Recently (as I write this, it is 2021), I had a dream that Adam and I were out in the country somewhere by a small house. A loaded pickup truck was parked in the driveway. Among the stuff piled on the truck was a motorbike. Adam said it was his, so I told him to take it back. He lifted it off the truck as if it was weightless and jumped on it. "Follow me," he said.

At first he drove slowly, and I followed quickly behind him. We approached what looked like the opening of a cave with a square, wooden frame at the entrance. I followed him inside. It was nearing nightfall outside, and of course, it was dark inside the cave. I could only see due to the headlights on his motorbike leading the way.

Adam sped up and I couldn't keep pace with him. "Adam, wait for me!" I repeatedly called out to him. He rode out of sight. I blindly felt along the walls of the cave until suddenly I came to a halt. I felt a door in front of me and opened it up to a brightly-lit room filled with people of all ages.

One gentleman was looking my way, smiling. I apologized for walking into what looked like his living room. He told me everyone had to pass through here and pointed to a long stairway, indicating I needed to climb those as well. I climbed and climbed, still searching for Adam. I woke up feeling like someone close to me, or even I, was going to die soon. It was very unnerving.

Joe shared a dream he had about Adam that put a smile on our faces. Back when the kids were younger, he said it drove him nuts that they would never simply sit down on furniture, but rather fell into it with obnoxious bouncing movements. In his dream, Adam showed up in our bedroom, greeted his dad, and fell into the bed just like he did when he was alive. They both laughed.

That dream tells me that Adam is saying not to sweat the small stuff. Or that furniture is replaceable, but people are not. Or maybe he just wanted to bring a smile to his father's face.

Chapter 4
Cardinals and Hearts

The day Adam died, we were all obviously in shock. However, signs that he had passed on and found peace were already there, although the impact of it all wouldn't hit us until months later. On the day he died, there was snow covering our back deck, the yard, and the tree branches beyond the trail behind our house. We had never seen a cardinal there before, yet on that particular day, there were several in the yard, on the branches and on the deck. One male in particular sat on the rail of the deck staring at us. I had always heard that when loved ones passed, they often sent cardinals to let you know they were okay. There were males and females everywhere! Did the entire family send us cardinals?

Joe had said when we had this house built in 2012, that he was drawn to this particular site by unseen forces. He felt that our grandparents and other loved ones who had passed on had picked this spot for us, and it felt right. Could it be that they knew what was coming for us? Did they know we would receive the confirmation we sought in this place? Were they all gathered there with Adam to give us extra reassurance because his was such a traumatic death? At so young an age and out of the order of things as we had expected life to be?

The cardinals have remained to this day. During the late fall after Adam passed away, Joe bought feeders and a water dish for them. It makes no difference whether we feed them or not (storms have knocked the feeders down from time to time), there is an entire family we see day to day. Blue jays, blackbirds, and a lone woodpecker, among other varieties, hang around, too, all year long!

Cardinals began to show up in other places, too. My brother Martin had one show up following Adam's death that would hang around on their back patio. Martin had a long, wide trellis surrounding the patio with vines climbing on it. He loves to grill, and he'd grill out back with the cardinal in the trellis bossing him around! He told me he was sassy!

My sister Ann's middle son, Tad, also lives with mental illness. He served time due to choices he made under the influence of alcohol and drugs, both of which can be a deadly combination with any mental illness. After Adam's death, stories began to surface of other family members having mental illness, showing the possibility of a genetic component to this problem.

Tad reached out to Adam from prison while he was recovering from his coma at Meadowbrook Rehabilitation Center in 2013. He wrote him letters and drew the most beautiful, inspiring pictures. After Tad was released, he spent some time at my mom's house. Mom was in a nursing home at the time, and my youngest sister, Kristina, was living there. Kristina, Ann, and son Tad were visiting. Tad called me on the phone. He was feeling sad and lamented that his choices had kept him from being there when Adam needed him and when he died. He had been unable to attend the funeral services of his own father, his grandfather, (my father) and his close cousin, Adam. I told him they were all at peace, and understanding and watching over him.

I told him about the cardinals. "You never know, Tad. He might send one your way," I said.

At that very second Tad began yelling loudly for his mom to come out to the back porch where he was sitting. Listening on the other end of the phone, I was wondering if everything was okay. He was telling her about our conversation, and they were both making sounds of awe. Finally, he returned to the conversation, breathless to tell me that the second I mentioned Adam sending a cardinal his way, one actually flew into the screened-in porch through a hole in the screen.

During May 2016, some friends, Ted Wilkens and his son Tyler, rented a double room at Big Cedar Lodge in Branson, Missouri. The rooms were connected and both had complete kitchens in them. Ted offered the second room to us for a really low price. The March before, Joe and I had purchased a Harley Road King (an "emotional purchase", we called it), and wanted to take it on a journey. Here was our opportunity, and we couldn't pass it up. Plus, I could see Tyler throughout the week as a bonus.

So we took him up on the offer. We rode the bike on long road trips during the day, exploring areas of southern Missouri and Arkansas. One day we rode to an area of the Buffalo River, where we had taken Stephanie and Adam canoeing with other family members back when they were kids.

During March 2016, Joe had reluctantly taken his annual "man float", a trip he'd been taking with a group of guys for many years. It was so close to Adam's passing that he wasn't sure he felt right about it, but I encouraged him to go, and it ended up being a good thing for him. On that trip, he went to a particular spot, reached into the water, and pulled out a heart-shaped rock about the size of the palm of his hand. He had been thinking of Adam when that happened. (You see, not just cardinals showed up, but coins and hearts as well).

After he took me to this same exact spot and told me about it, he took off his shoes and socks, rolled up his jeans, and walked out to the place where he'd found the rock. He reached his hand down into the water and pulled out another heart-shaped rock! This one was the size of a nickel!

Our dear friends Jim and Jeanne Finnegan, who now live in Arizona, sent us a plaque in honor of Adam. On the plaque it read:

God saw you getting tired
A cure was not to be,
So He put his arms around you
And Whispered, "come with me."
With tearful eyes we watched you
And saw you fade away,
Although we loved you dearly,
We could not make you stay.
A golden heart stopped beating
Your tender hands at rest.
God took you home to prove to us,
He only takes the best.

The very day that plaque arrived, I went to drive the car. On the ground outside the driver's side door was a gold-colored heart, like it had fallen off of a necklace!

Another friend, Julie Easely, who had worked closely with Joe for twenty years in Tulsa, sent me a necklace with the inscription: "God had you in his arms, I have you in my heart." Attached to the chain was a heart!

So, here we were on this motorcycle trip in Arkansas. Cardinals literally crossed our path several times! We headed back to Big Cedar. Joe purposefully passed the lodge, even though we had been riding a good eight or nine hours. "Can you humor me?" he asked. "I feel like driving down this road. Maybe fifteen to twenty minutes more?"

I agreed. We headed one direction, then turned around and

headed back. I wish I had my phone/camera on hand, but I'd kept it in the saddle bags so I wouldn't drop it. I looked to my right and saw a mailbox with a wrought iron decoration on the top. It was red, and it was a cardinal! But that wasn't all! Right next to it was a road sign, "Adam's Road!"

My friend, Beck Beers from NAMI Family Support Group, was traveling away from home that year. She was worried about her son, who was staying at home alone. She asked Adam to watch over him, and a cardinal appeared! She took a picture of it and sent it to me right away! Then she walked into a gift shop (during the summer) and there, right in front of her, was a small, lone Christmas ornament of a cardinal! Of course, she knew she had to buy if for me! Ever since then, she picks up random items with cardinals on them for me, but I am convinced that on this particular trip it was a sign from above.

Almost immediately after Adam died, I began packing up his things and giving them away. Kristina gently asked me if I was sure about doing this so soon. I knew people who kept the bedrooms of their loved ones who had passed on exactly the same, even leaving dirty laundry strewn about on the floor. I was worried about being that person.

I'm not sure really what I was thinking during those days, but Adam's loved ones were there. They all loved him and he loved them. Something told me they needed a part of him to take with them. Adam's nephew, William, was the same size in clothing and shoes. He took many of Adam's pants and sweaters and some shoes. Joe kept some of his dress shoes, as he wore the same size shoe.

Adam had some nice clothes. He was fascinated with shoes and jackets. His niece Jessica took a jacket that was unisex-looking, a sailor style, spring jacket. Others took coats, and Joe kept a few. I kept a lot of hoodies. Adam was small, and that was one thing I could fit. We gave some of his knickknacks away to others. His niece Addie took a newer hoodie of his that she later gave to her mom because she grew very tall! Aunt Debbie wanted a pair of his socks and wears them during the winter (indoors, because they are big on her tiny feet) when she is missing him and feels his love warm her. My brother Martin asked to take his T-shirts because his mother-in-law, Nancy, could make pillows out of them. However, her husband, Bob became seriously ill, and her attention was focused on caring for him until he passed away.

So at some point, Martin took the shirts to an old friend, Kris Remus, who had also lost a son. She knew a lady in Missouri named Jennifer Burnett, who had lost her daughter to a rare genetic disorder, Cornelia De Lange Syndrome. She is a registered nurse who works in delivery, getting to enjoy helping mostly healthy babies come into the world. Prior to that, she worked in the intensive care unit, watching children die. It had been very taxing on her.

Anyway, this wonderful lady took on the shirts of our son, whom she had never even knew, and she made two quilts, one for Joe and one for me. In addition, she took a piece of Adam's artwork, made a square out of it, framed it, and gave it to Joe.

We went to meet her early on, before her quilts were completed. I was in awe that this lady, a total stranger, would do this for us so selflessly, while she was grieving herself. She lives out in the country in New Franklin, Missouri, on a gravel road in a beautiful two-story house. We immediately loved her and have been friends ever since. (Coincidentally, her daughter's name was Kelsi, which is a family name of ours, Kelsey.)

The day we met we talked about signs from heaven. I talked about the cardinals, and she sadly told me she looks for them every day and has never seen one since Kelsi's death, even though she lives in the country. As we were leaving, pulling out of her driveway onto the gravel road, two cardinals flew right in front of our car, a male and a female! I immediately messaged Jennifer.

She was so excited! "They know each other in heaven!" she exclaimed. "They found each other, and they are wanting us to know they are okay!" we both agreed.

Every year following the Christmas holidays, I go up and down the basement stairs, carrying boxes of decorations down to storage. Yes, we still celebrate Christmas. To pass up the holiday Adam died on would do him a dishonor, not to mention God himself. Each year I experience the same thing heading down those stairs. I will hear a knocking noise. I look at the windows, and in one, a male cardinal is in the window box repeatedly flying into the window. I know they commonly see their reflections and dive into window panes. However, why, in this box that basically sits underground, and why on this particular day every year? If I call out, "Hey, Adam! I know you are with me! I get it! Please make the cardinal stop before he gets hurt!" it will promptly fly away.

During 2020, Marlon (Stephanie's boyfriend) lost his job during the Coronavirus pandemic. The same week, we had torrential rains, and his car was flooded at his job. It was in the shop getting repaired due to damage from the flooding. I was on my way to pick up Stephanie to run an errand with Nick and Sadie in the back seat (the two kids I am nanny to). On the way there, six different times, a male cardinal flew in front of the car. Suddenly, Sadie said, "Look at the sky, Heidi. The cloud looks like a bird with a worm in his mouth." I felt at peace that everything would work out for them—that a new life chapter would emerge and it would be better than before.

In August 2020, I saw our male cardinal on the trail behind our house. His movements were shaky. I knew he was dying. That was the last time I saw him. I missed our friend. One day in October, I was walking our dog, Bentley, on the trail. I said aloud, "Adam, I really miss the cardinal you sent me. It would be okay if you sent another one."

That very moment, a male cardinal flew in front of us! I laughed and said, "Okay, showoff! Send me a flock!" I rounded the next corner, and five or six cardinals flew in front of us! I went home to no cardinals. The next day I said, "It would be okay if you sent a new one to our home." Since that day, I have had a new male and female, and they both rap on the window like the old one did! When people say the only reason the cardinal hits the window is because he thinks he sees another male and is fighting for a female's attention, I have to chuckle. With our newest pair, it is the female who does this, and she is very dramatic. She will fly into the window and plaster herself against it with her wings spread out looking frantically at us. I tell her to move along and she will, but she always comes back to repeat her behavior.

Chapter 5
Other Signs from Heaven

Besides cardinals and hearts, Joe, Stephanie, and I, along with other family members, have seen other signs from Heaven. Shortly after Adam's passing, we could sense him everywhere. While planning his Celebration of Life, my sisters and Joe's sister were dragging up pictures from the basement to put in the video presentation that Debbie put together and the picture collages that Ann put together to display on the tables.

There was one picture in particular that was sitting on the bar. Joe and I were talking to Debbie and my sisters, when suddenly, a picture rose off of the counter and flew in our direction (a few feet), landing on the floor at our feet. We all stood silently for a moment, and then someone joked, saying maybe Adam was telling us to put that picture in the display, or maybe he was saying he didn't like that one! Or maybe...he was showing us that he was with us.

We felt like we could smell him for months, even down to cigarette smoke on his clothing, except it wasn't as offensive as it was in real life. I could feel him touching my face or moving his hand through my hair when I felt sad. At times, I still do. Or I will feel chills run up my legs, arms and spine.

The first Mother's Day after his death, I was at my cousin Gary's church in Columbia, and I could feel my legs give out underneath me. I promptly felt arms around me, lifting me back up and holding me in place. I felt a sense of calm and peace come over me. No one I could actually see was doing this. Was this Adam? Or was it God Himself?

Twice, I saw Adam in my room during the night. The first time he was sitting on a stool beside my bed. I woke up, saw him, was startled, and screamed. He disappeared immediately. I told him I was sorry. I really wanted to see him. It was just unexpected, and it frightened me.

Shortly after this, he appeared again. I had been lying awake, unable to sleep, and there he was sitting right beside me on the bed. I wasn't afraid this time. He sat wearing a hoodie, which was common while he was living, its hood pulled over his head. His face was tilted downward. I looked at his profile. I stared for a moment, not wanting to scare him away again. I said, "Adam, l love you, and I miss you." I reached up to caress his face, and he left, just as fast as he had come.

My niece Jessica sees Adam often. So does Stephanie. They both have spiritual gifts that I cannot explain that open them up to these visits. Jessica told me about a move she had made. She was packing boxes and sat down to rest on top of one along a wall that bordered another wall. She glanced up, and there he was on the other side of the bend of the wall! He was grinning from ear to ear! Another time, she was in her kitchen, and he walked across her living room in front of her! She says the visits continue to this day but assures me he hangs around Stephanie, Joe, and me the most.

Stephanie has had experiences with things being moved. She has pictures of Adam arranged a certain way that she did not touch, as if they were sacred or something. Yet, she would leave the room and return to find them completely turned around, when no one was home except for her! Stephanie has a drawer she leaves alone because it contains items from loved ones who have passed: Mimi (Joe's mom), Papa (my father), my mom, and Adam. She told me of times she went to take a shower, and when she returned, that drawer would be opened wide.

My brother Martin and his wife Angie had a strange occurrence between Adam's death and a week later at his funeral services. They went home briefly to pack some things. In their bedroom that night, the blinds behind their bed began to open and close on their own. There were no vents or fans nearby, and the windows were sealed for the winter. At one point, Angie called out, "Okay, Adam! Knock it off!" It stopped. They also received a random call from a stranger, whose voice sounded like Adam.

We had a tall dresser in our room. On top of it was a heavy Longaberger basket, which sat at the back away from the edge. On one occasion, Joe walked into the room, and it moved right in front of him to the floor. As Joe told the story, he tried to reenact the scene. He had only walked by it before, when the basket fell. He jumped up and down, making movements that should have made it fall, and it didn't! During April 2016, Joe, Stephanie, and I attended an event put on by Suicide Awareness Survivor Support-Missouri/Kansas. We had attended one meeting for survivors close to home but had never gone back. Maybe it was too soon. We still hadn't processed the suicide. I don't know why, but it didn't work for us. It made me feel hopeless hearing people who had lost loved ones many years before still feeling stuck on that day.

SASS hosts these Healing Days every spring and during the holidays of winter, and holds an annual suicide remembrance walk. We attend these as often as possible. We participated in our first walk with Adam by our side during the fall of 2015 in remembrance of Clayton Hugill, the son of our dear friends, Clay and Annette. Clayton had died by suicide the previous April. Now we attend for both of them.

The first spring following Adam's death, we attended Healing Day. There were massages, art therapy, soft music, and more. There was a lady there, one of the speakers of the day, who suddenly blurted out during her speech that she was very distracted because she could see the spirits of our loved ones all around the room, including our pets! It was very unsettling. Later, when we were milling around, Stephanie and I went up to talk to her. It was then that we realized she had a gift for sure. She described Adam perfectly and said he was right there with us holding a very fat cat. She described our beloved Fred! She told us things she couldn't have known.

She said, "There is another family member in this room who is a talented musician, he says. Where is he?"

We pointed across the room to Joe. She told us to turn on the radio when we got into the car. Adam would be sending us a message through the very first song we would hear. It was "That's All," by Phil Collins. At first I thought, Why this unlikely song? However, as I listened to the words I had heard hundreds of times over the years, I got it! Wow! So Adam! I feel like it was Adam trying to tell us how we felt, and some of it was true, even though it hurts to admit that. In the words of a song that sounds upbeat, you realize the person singing it is not doing okay and feels he is being a burden to others.

These are a few of the signs we witnessed that assured us that our boy passed over and is safe. I will share more of them as I tell of how we have gone on to live the legacy of our precious son, Adam. While the miracles, as we saw them, through cardinals, hearts, dreams, and sightings occurred throughout the years since Adam's death, I would like to share other elements of our journey and moving ahead in our lives, as difficult as it has been. As I write, I can see how every occurrence on this journey has been linked together somehow: the people, the places, the miracles, and a journey that eventually gave us our lives back in a powerful way.

Some of you reading this story have your own story to tell. You may be new at this or already well-traveled down this road. I want to impart upon you that how you feel is part of the process, and I want you to know that you are not alone in the journey you now face. Please don't shut people out! You need them now, and you will need them later.

You might say that you don't want to recover. That you don't care anymore. That you want to join your loved one. I know from experience that we all have these feelings, and while it is true that you will never "get over it", you can at least find a way to walk with it, and you need people to do that.

There is an overwhelming love that occurs as a result of tragedy—from family and friends of the bereaved coming together and guiding them through their dark times, to the people who take care of their physical needs, like meal preparation. Without these people, it would be hard for the bereaved to survive this ordeal, and how would that honor their loved one's name and life?

Chapter 6
Stages of Grief

I remember learning about the five stages of grief in psychology class, way back in my college days. I remember thinking that those would never apply to me because I was young, and everyone I knew would die of old age, and when it happened, I would automatically accept it. However, now, three-and-a-half years after Adam's death as I write this chapter, I have a better understanding of the stages of loss and know where I stand.

Denial. Wow, did we go through denial both during Adam's life and after his death. We denied Adam's illness for so long, and once he was gone, we couldn't believe that he really was. We figured that he had died before and returned to us, so maybe if we would just go to sleep one night, it would all turn out to be a nightmare, and we would wake up and he would be with us again, whole, and well. Even today, I wake up some mornings, open my eyes, look out my window at the trees, and think, "Wow. It really happened. It wasn't a bad dream. Adam really left us."

Anger. At whom? At what? Joe and I both agree that we never felt anger at Adam and his choice to leave us. We were angry at the world. At God. At ourselves. Why did it seem like everyone else we knew in the world had healthy, well-adjusted children who got to live life without so much pain? Where was the fairness? Why us? What kind of God gives you a child to love and raise, then makes him so sick that he wants to die, and then takes him from you? Your only son. However, the biggest load of anger was self-directed. Why did we leave him that night? Why didn't we see the signs that he was going to do this again? This feeling of guilt followed our self-directed anger. Guilt should be considered a stage of grief. Guilt for things we said in the past, for things we did or didn't do. Joe blames himself. I blame myself.

In 2014, Adam lost his Zyprexa, a mood stabilizer he would take in the event that the voices in his head returned. He couldn't purchase a new bottle for over two months because he had a three-month supply that he had just purchased a couple of weeks prior. He told me he didn't need it anyway, and by the way things looked, it seemed that he was right. Now my thoughts (to this day) are that I killed him. I killed my son, by not pursuing a new prescription, even if it cost me a few hundred dollars out of pocket. I just let it go. He was never on it again until he relapsed in July 2015. What if he had remained on that pill? Was that what was keeping him sane all that time? I will never know. I will carry that guilt to my own grave.

Bargaining. Why do we do this one? Seriously, I have sometimes hoped that if I prayed hard enough, then I would go to sleep, and when I woke up Adam would be back, and life would be great. Truthfully, we do this when we are drowning in grief! As stupid as it sounds, we do it. Joe and I just wanted our lives back. We wanted to be happy and to live like everyone else. Why couldn't we have that?

Depression. This is not like clinical depression, but rather it is a feeling as low as life can feel and a loss that seems to go on forever. Every now and then, something good will happen, and you will feel a slight hope that life will be okay again, but then you slip under again. You feel you cannot experience happiness or joy without that dreaded guilt again. "How can I be happy when my boy felt nothing but pain? It's not right or fair."

When your child dies by suicide (or dies period), the thought of getting out of bed in the morning is unbearable. You really want to go to sleep and never wake up again. To feel the pain over and over is more than you think you can take. If you have to go to work, you have to force yourself up and out. You struggle to smile and act normal until you can get into your car again and scream and cry all the way home.

This is our reality. It can literally go on for years. Then one day you realize that although it can hit you again many times, it lessens over time. You find a way to navigate around the pain or to hold it in a special box in your heart to revisit every now and then. You learn to find a little bit of joy, too, and that is where you find acceptance.

Acceptance. Will I ever really accept the fact that Adam is dead? I can't truthfully answer that question because accepting it totally feels like giving up on him and losing him forever. Acceptance for me is knowing that he passed away, but that he is with God, is happy, and is free of pain and illness. I can accept that. I can accept the belief that he is with me every day and is with all of his loved ones, watching over us until we meet again. And what a joyous day that will be.

Chapter 7
Trying to Find a New "Normal"

2016: Before Adam's funeral services, Joe and I went to NA-MI's Kansas City office. Nikk Thompson worked there and asked us into his office. Nikk had graduated from Lee's Summit High School in 1969. He had been accepted into West Point Academy but had suddenly decided to join the 173rd Airborne Brigade and left for Vietnam in 1970.

After returning, he received many Letters of Commendations from the Department of the Army Headquarters. He served as a liaison non-commissioned officer at Fort Ord, California, where he assisted in fine tuning the Special Unit Enlistment program implemented by the 101st Airborne Division, which became an effective and highly successful all-volunteer force. Nikk received an outstanding Commendation for leadership. He also taught at the West Point Academy in 1972 and received a Letter of Appreciation from Colonel Richard L. Gruenther, Infantry, Director of Military Instruction, for outstanding performance in instructing, evaluating and advising cadets, and for platoon and company tactical training.

In 1976, he earned his Associate Degree of Applied Science at Longview Community College. In 1984, he worked and trained non-commission officers in Jefferson City, Missouri. He was a decorated police officer, who served the Lee's Summit Police Department for 27 years from 1980 to 2007. He worked many years as a detective, as well as a hostage negotiator. In 1998, Nikk earned a Bachelor Degree in Bible and Organizational Leadership at Calvary Bible College. In

2006, he earned his Master's Degree in Christian Studies from the Calvary Theological Seminary.

Nikk was a big part of the Crisis Intervention Team program Joe and I spoke at. He was responsible for starting the C.I.T. for the Lee's Summit Police Department. That initiative spread throughout the metro area and all across the state of Missouri and into Kansas. He was nominated for his work as Jackson County's Most Influential Person, and his name was inscribed on a plaque that hangs in the downtown Jackson County Courthouse beside other prestigious names, including President Harry Truman.

We met Nikk during our first C.I.T. presentation. He put us at ease then and later on the day we walked into NAMI KC after Adam died. Nikk was a Christian man and wanted to talk to us to make sure we were okay. He spoke of where our boy was and gave us a lot of peace. He asked Joe, who looked so pained and lost, "Do you want Adam back, Joe?" Of course he did, Joe replied. Nikk asked him if he believed Adam no longer suffered in Heaven and that he was happy. Joe agreed that he believed that this was true. "So, you would want him to come back to this suffering here?" In a gentle way, he put a whole new twist on things.

God rest Nikk Thompson's soul, as he followed Adam shortly thereafter in August 2016. He had some health issues that took him. He was kind and gentle—a major player in NAMI who will be forever missed.

ReDiscover was insistent that we see a counselor there, too. We did, although I cannot remember his name. I just remember that Joe and I raised our eyebrows at each other when we left. It was a quick session. The counselor pulled out a sheet of paper with all the stages of grief inside the picture of a brain, all mixed together. He simply asked us at what stage we felt we were in. Adam had JUST died. We were in all of them!

As we left, Joe said, "They did their job. They wanted to feel us out to make sure we didn't hold ReDiscover accountable and file a lawsuit."

"Why would we do that?" I asked. After all, they'd done all they could.

"Just covering bases, that's all," he replied.

That baffled me. No doctor is perfect. None of us are. For the most part, I think ReDiscover had Adam's best interests at heart and treated him to the best of their ability.

Right after the funeral services, Ann and Debbie stayed with us for a week to make sure we were going to be okay. It really helped. The week following that, my brother, Jimmy, and Suzanne invited us to Richland, Missouri, to get away for a time. They live out in the country, and the fresh air and change of scenery did us a bit of good. Their sweet girls, Kataryna and Ahreanna, sat with me on the floor of their bedroom and cried with me when I broke down.

Two weeks after Adam passed away, Joe and I both returned to work. I know people who never return to their occupations or take months to do so. My family still seemed so lost, and that frightened me. I needed to do something to keep myself busy, so I wasn't all consumed with horrific thoughts. For me, the children whom I nanny were a great outlet. Children are generally happy, loving, and kind, yet those two have a built-in radar as far as I am concerned. Craig and Lisa Peterson, the parents of, the two children I nanny for, are very honest and open with their children. As a result, the children are very adaptable, relaxed, and laid-back. They don't fear many things because they confront them early on.

I appreciate that because I am the same way. As a young child, I went to many family's and friends' funeral services. I accepted death as a normal part of life. Nick and Sadie, the Peterson children, attended the visitation. Sadie was only one at the time, so she probably doesn't remember much, but Nick was almost four. He remembers. He is compassionate, and to this day if I have a "moment, he asks, "Is it Adam?" and he hugs me. His mom will warn him that on anniversaries or holidays, I might have a rough day. He has always been in tune, and now Sadie is, too.

So, while the laughter, fun, and games with the children keep me going and filled with hope for the future, these little people are also my comfort during rough patches.

The NAMI Walk, which Adam had encouraged me to do, became something real for me very soon after he died. I had already decided, at his urging, to do the walk in early December 2015. Our walk planning committee was formed, and planning began late January 2016, four weeks after his death. Looking back, I am not sure how I did that, but I did have a great team of volunteers who joined in the effort. We had tremendous support from NAMI-Missouri's then-Executive Director, Cindi Keele Johnson, whom we dearly love within and outside of the organization. The Missouri office is in Jefferson City, but Cindi was consistently available to us to answer questions and guide us along. Our organization in Kansas City was failing financially, and she did everything she could to help keep us afloat.

Our NAMI Walk goal was to raise money to save our city affiliate. Usually, you buy into the NAMI walks, but our affiliate couldn't afford to do that, so I researched fundraisers and walks and basically came up with my own agenda. I had never taken on something like this before but kept hearing Adam in my head saying, "You can do this,

Mom!" Cindi gave us the go-ahead to do this without NAMI's support. We couldn't call it NAMI walks, but we could raise money for the organization. We called it March for Mental Health. My team included my co-chair, Tyler Sharpe, who had been Adam's clinical case worker at ReDiscover when he passed away. (Adam and all of us had just fallen in love with Tyler.)

He had the inside connections working in the mental health field to obtain sponsorship for us, and he did a brilliant job. The rest of my team consisted of people who were part of my support group during that time: Clay and Annette Hugill, Cathy Simonds (she also taught Family to Family with Joe), Charles French, Joe Custin, Lisa Ann Bailey, Sarah Caldwell, and I have to save these two for last: Isabelle Abaar and Kristen Springer, who have my back at every turn.

In addition to my planning team, I had several volunteers for event day, including my dear friend Elizabeth Wilson (who is my photographer at all my events), and Richard Bennet (who also has lived experience and is a phenomenal advocate like Elizabeth). They both inspire me as people who can prove to others that a person can live a full life while dealing with mental illness and serve as true friends and support to those who need it. Winging it on a walk fundraiser is no easy feat, but with these people and determination, we knew we would be able to pull it off.

Craig and Leslie Jones, my friends who live in Texas, own a T-shirt company called Groggy Dog. They cater to sports teams for the most part, but they worked with us on our first year shirts, donating the shirts that Team Adam wore and discounting the rest of the shirts. The walk was set for early October.

In January 2016, my friend Tracy Young called me to ask me to join her women's Bible Study group, the M&M's, named for Mary and Martha, the two sisters of Lazarus in the New Testament. Tracy and I have known each other for over thirty years now. When I met Joe, Tracy, her husband Brad, and Joe all worked for State Farm Insurance. We were all single at the time. Eventually, Joe and I got married, and so did Brad and Tracy. When the regional office opened in 1989 in Tulsa, Oklahoma, we all transferred there, along with many other people we knew. Later, Brad and Tracy moved to the Kansas City area, where Brad became a field underwriter. Tracy now works from home, teaching webinar classes to State Farm agents and executives.

When Tracy invited me to join her group, she told me that she had been facilitating this group study for years. The women who attended mostly came from her Methodist Church in Pleasant Hill, Missouri. There were a few from other churches, even one who was Catholic. I was raised Methodist and had been a practicing Catholic for a good twenty-five years, so I thought it would work for me. She also told me that the women felt they knew me because they had been following our story since 2012 and praying for Adam and our family. She also let me in on a secret: while Joe and I had been praying for a peaceful passing when Adam was removed from life support, they had been praying for life. They were every bit a part of the miracle.

Of course, I joined the M&M's. It is a thirty-minute drive for me, so there are times I cannot attend. Joe has to drive because the trek is on curvy country roads, and my night vision is horrible. He spends time with Brad and their dog Daisy (who is in love with Joe) while the rest of us meet. If Joe is working out of town or roads are bad during the winter, I don't attend, but these ladies have in some form or another been a lifeline to our family. Tracy is one of those connections I wrote about in *Adam's Contract With God*. Thirty-plus years ago, I couldn't imagine the impact that little lady would have on my life and in my world. She was even the one who arranged the church for Adam's services, since we hadn't yet established ourselves in a church since our move. We had mostly been going to Columbia and attending Newman Center with Joe's parents, although occasionally we'd attend my cousin Gary's Church of the Revolution.

After the lack of support I received from the Catholic Church, I wasn't feeling it there anymore, but we knew that we needed to get back into some church. We visited several throughout the Kansas City area, but none of them had that feeling we were looking for. We were so exhausted from grief during this time and just trying to get through each day, that adding church into the mix actually seemed an exhausting thought to me. So, I did the next best thing I could do at the time, and I joined these ladies.

What a wonderful mix of delightful, loving women. They would later be my inspiration for getting back into the church. In February 2016, I volunteered to go to Nick's Valentine's Day party at his preschool, taking Sadie, who was fourteen months old at the time, along. I didn't know it until that day, but going to those kinds of things are triggers for me. I felt like I had an out-of-body experience. I was standing frozen in place, kids milling around me, blowing bubbles, bouncing balloons, singing and dancing on the little stage. It took me back to my own preschool in Broken Arrow, "Heidi's Home for Early Learning, Inc." I envisioned my own two mixed in with the others at this age. I saw little boys who had blond hair and blue eyes like my little Adam bobbing around. I started shaking, trying to hold it together. I couldn't control the tears that started to fall. I felt humiliated and very alone while all this happiness flowed around me but couldn't touch me. The tears I couldn't control kept flowing.

A mom immediately came to me and asked if I was okay. Of

course that only made it worse. I can usually hold back a while until some kind, compassionate soul comes along and asks if I am okay. Then the dam bursts. I told her this was difficult because I'd had a preschool of my own years before that my own children had been a part of. I told her that my son had died seven weeks before. I apologized. She looked at me like she was wondering why I was apologizing. She hugged me and asked me to tell her about Adam. What a sweetheart!

Those of us who lose children desire so much to speak of them, just like those with living children like to speak of theirs. They were and are still a part of us, and talking about them keeps them alive in our hearts. When I told her my story, she cried and told me she'd had a suicide in her family, too. I have since discovered that when I open up to strangers, often through wearing a shirt with logos about mental health or suicide prevention, that many have a story to tell themselves. It is part of my mission in life to stomp out stigma, because the more we talk about it, the less scary it is. As a result, people who live with mental illness or have suicidal thoughts might be more likely to find help.

We also attempted a support group for suicide survivors in February. I met a lady named Lisa Cable on Facebook, through Adam's good friend Nikki Riley. She had lost her son to suicide, too. She didn't really attend the meetings anymore but went to support Joe and me. That meant so much to me. I have learned a lot about her, mostly through Facebook, since we only attended the group one time. It was too painful at the time to go more often. Lisa doesn't even know it, but she is an inspiration to me, as are all the mothers and fathers like us. We are all connected, members in a club none of us asked to join. Like my friend Clay Hugill once said, "I am happy I know you, but hate the reason why I do."

In March, we made the "emotional" motorcycle purchase I

mentioned earlier. We had been riding on a little 1992 Harley Sportster, so it made sense. It was way more comfortable for longer rides, and we did enjoy our ride to Branson and into Arkansas in June.

Also in March, I had a rough night (one of many). It was storming pretty badly outside. I woke up during the wee hours of the morning missing my son, as usual. It was around his birthday, his first birthday in Heaven, away from me, his mama. I ached for him with every fiber of my being. I laid on my side in bed staring out the window at the trees along the trail behind our house. I thought of that song I mentioned in *Adam's Contract with God*, John Denver's "For Baby". I softly sang to myself: "I'll walk in the rain by your side...little birds will sing along in time..." I thought of the rain, of all the birds that had shown up since he died. When I sang the words, "leaves will bow down when you walk by", the tree limbs outside all suddenly blew over to one side so violently I thought they might break. But gently, they swayed up the other way and stopped!

"Thank you, thank you!" I cried. "Adam, I gave that song to you so many years ago, and now you are giving it back to me. You are showing me in your way that you are okay and alive in spirit. I WILL see you again!" The storm didn't frighten me. It gave me peace.

In April, we took a spur-of-the-moment cruise with Princess Cruises. We had gone on several cruises with family and friends in the past with Carnival Cruise Line, but we decided that this one was to be just for the two of us. We needed to get away and sort out life as we knew it, and yes, grieve away from the prying eyes of others.

We took a California Coast Cruise. At each port, we got out and did our own thing, mostly walking long distances (as we love to do anyway), checking out each port on our own. We visited my niece Brittney and her husband Byron, who were in the Air Force and stationed in the San Francisco area. We got to see their two boys, Jude and baby Jonah. (Ahh, we needed that baby therapy, too!)

We talked for hours on our trip, loved on one another, laughed, and cried. We drank a lot of coffee and had midday desserts with that at tea time. We exercised a lot, too, and enjoyed the crisp, clean air. We vowed that this tragedy, like any other thing, would never tear us apart. Thank God, Joe and I are strong in that way.

We sure needed that break as May rolled around. Joe was president of the board of NAMI-KC. Things were looking pretty bad. I felt sorry for Joe, as he had walked into a mess that he was unaware of. He so wanted to save our chapter, the one that had done so much for us. Many of the people we loved who worked there had already left or were let go due to decreased funding (common in the mental health field). Our Executive Director was nearing retirement, and we tried to hang on for her sake and for the sake of all those people who had pulled us through. We dearly loved them, but we had to let them down, or all of us would suffer dire consequences.

The last day of May, our office shut down. We had a NAMI KC vigil at a park witnessed by news cameras. Joe spoke, broken-hearted. He had lost his son, and now this. Unfortunately, comments made by the media and other people led many folks around the city to believe that there would be no NAMI at all in Kansas City—no support groups and no classes. Jim and Joan Smith, the couple responsible for starting the KC chapter thirty-six years earlier, were devastated. We'd had the privilege of meeting them at the picnic. They've had more than one child with mental illness and also had a son who had taken his life. I appreciated how proactive they were back in those days, when it seemed to me that no one talked about such things! It was up to us now to show them we could go on, for the memory of their son, and now for the memory of ours. We are forever indebted to this couple who gave us a place to turn to when we needed it most, even though we didn't get the chance to meet them until the shutdown.

Joe read "An Open Letter to a Person with Mental Illness", by Rachel Griffin. In her letter, Rachel speaks to someone who lives with mental illness. She speaks without judgment in her words, letting the person know they are neither a monster nor crazy. She speaks of the creative mind, how the mind of a creative works differently than those of others, and how it can be a beautiful thing. She speaks of how valuable that person is and how they can live in this world with a mental illness.

She lets them know how valuable they are as a human being. She compares mental illness to other illnesses like diabetes, the victims of which receive compassion for their illness. She takes away the self-blaming feelings. She encourages them to stay close to those who understand them and have compassion for them, instead of the negative people who don't. It reminded me of something Joe always told our kids: "Hang around the people who make you feel good." She encourages them to seek treatment. She speaks of dark and light times. Most importantly, she emphasizes that the person is not their illness and that they are worthy of love.

It isn't obvious until the end of the letter that Rachel is speaking from experience and also suffers from mental illness. What a powerful statement! Joe received so much positive feedback about that letter he read. It impacted us, too, wishing we had said those things to Adam.

I contacted Cindi Keele Johnson and asked what we should do about the walk now. She said, "Go on with it! You don't have to have an office or employees to run a nonprofit organization."

So, we continued with our walk planning, and we became NA-

MI-GKC (Greater Kansas City). Within the next year, we would realize how much NAMI meant to Kansas City. NAMI unloaded their office supplies and stored them in our basement for the next two-and-a-half years.

My friend, Tomas, is one of those powerfully supportive friends who pushes me to move when I feel down. He often sends me motivational messages by text or on Facebook. He kept encouraging Joe and I to get out and do something fun. He knows we volunteer a lot, but he wants us to live, too. After losing his sixteen-year-old sister to murder, he understands that feeling of loss. He also lives with mental illness and works to help other people who suffer from it. He is driven to help others who are experiencing similar pain, but he truly is a caring, great friend. He asked Joe and I to come to a cookout at his apartment pool. In June, we took him up on it. He has never let up on me or Joe, and I appreciate him so much.

It was Tomas who introduced me to Leanna Brunner, my editor. I met with her during the spring of 2016, feeling like I could write this book with her encouragement and her belief in my story and me. What I didn't realize at the time was that I was still in shock over Adam's death, and completion of the first book would not come until the winter of 2019. It was very traumatic to relive Adam's life, the good times and the bad, because my love for him is so great and the loss is overwhelming.

During August 2016, we went on a family canoeing trip. My sister Ann and all three of her boys—Christopher, Tad and Will—were together for the first time in years. Martin, Kristina, and a few of Christopher's friends from Tulsa came. Joe and I brought "Lil' Man", Marlon Peters, Jr., son of our daughter Stephanie's boyfriend. Lil' Man identified us as Pop'z and Nana, and we loved playing grandparents to this nine-year-old boy and providing new experiences for him. It had been heartbreaking to think that we would never have grandkids, and then suddenly, he came into our world.

We also brought my beloved friend, Michael Brown, the artist I introduced in *Adam's Contract with God*. Neither of them had ever camped or canoed. Unfortunately, even though it was August in Missouri, it was rainy and cold. Lil' Man didn't care for that too much, but Michael just loved every moment of it. This is something I love about Michael. He can enter into any situation and soak in the moment, turning it into a learning experience. I owe a great deal to Michael for all the days and nights he corresponded with me in my despair. A true friend. He is one who will tell it like it is and wastes no time letting someone know if they are walking down the wrong road. He gave me so much grace. I kept waiting for the moment he would say, "Enough is enough; get over it already."

Prior to the float trip, my firstborn nephew Christopher sent me a message saying he needed to tell me something. He is not one to attend church or to talk about life after death, and I don't pressure him to. He lived with our family in Broken Arrow for a few years before we moved, enduring much of our children's teenage years along with us. He is six years older than Stephanie, and it hurt him a lot to see what we went through. He also lived with me for a short time when he was four and his mother was going through a divorce.

Christopher's message to me was this: "Please don't ask any questions. I am only the messenger. I was sleeping one night recently in my house and had to get up to use the bathroom and get a drink of water. I had to leave my room and pass through the living room to reach the kitchen for the water. Right there on my couch sat Adam. He chuckled and said, 'I bet you are surprised to see me.' I said aloud to him, 'I am just wondering what kind of hallucinogens I have to be on to see you here.' He told me he had an important message to deliver to his parents. He wanted to tell you to chill and stop worrying. He is doing great." Chris said he didn't know what we were worrying about, but that was the message. We had plenty to worry about. Adam was gone and we couldn't find him and felt so much pain and guilt. However, through hearing stories like this, we go on believing he is alive and well. Chris said, "Believe me or don't believe me. That was the message."

I believed! I asked Chris what the color of his shirt was, and he said, "I told you, no questions." I had to laugh. I felt that Adam had chosen the most unlikely person to believe in his life after death. He was working through Chris to give us hope. Of course, it worked!

Also in August 2016, Joe set up a private plane ride for Lil' Man and the two of us with one of his fellow State Farm agents. It gave us great joy to see another thrilling, first-time event for this young boy. I relate these events in this book because I feel it is important to go on living and doing things in life that can bring you some joy, and I know that Adam would want that for us. Experiencing this joy through this young boy put life back into us. Every choice we made to get involved with something honored Adam and helped us on the road to recovery. We will never get over it, but through these experiences, we learn to live through it.

Sometimes it was things we really didn't want to do or have the emotional energy to do, like an outdoor concert we went to that month with our friends, Brad and Tracy Young, and Tony and Karen Kehrees. We dragged ourselves out and actually enjoyed our friends' company. They, along with many others who were in our lives or came into our lives later, would continue to do this. My advice to those in our shoes is to go along with these friends if you can muster the strength. It will strengthen you and keep you connected to the outside world.

In September, our family, Bob and Becky Beers, and Clay and Annette Hugill and their daughter Allie, went on the annual SASS walk. It was very emotional. We completed the walk first, and then the names of the suicide victims were read. How strange to hear our son's name on that list! All the women were given a carnation, and a Lionel Richie song, "Good-bye," was played. I can never get through the first line of that song without sobbing. Yes, I wanted him for life, as the song begins. It was very moving and a great choice for the event. They even released doves!

We interacted with the other families and realized we were not alone. Yes, it was a very emotional, touching ceremony. We also celebrated Stephanie's 26th birthday. We went bowling with her, Marlon, and her closest friend, Elizabeth Davis, her boyfriend, Chuck Compton, and Elizabeth's three children, Jassy, Ali, and Jack. They had all loved Adam and had spent quite a bit of time with him during his last few years of life. We made the most of it and had some fun, but the fact that Adam was absent hung over our heads.

During the summer months, our team worked hard to promote our walk. Finally, the day rolled around: October 9, 2016, the very first Kansas City walk for NAMI! I was a nervous wreck. I had to do a speech. I was concerned about the turnout. I was worried about the weather.

We held it at Berkley Riverfront Park in Kansas City, Missouri. It was chilly during the early morning setup, but we were hopeful it would warm up by the check-in time. We had so many volunteers for check-in, race monitoring, and food, water, and shirt distribution. My team had done a phenomenal job considering it was our first time! Kristen, a woman from my group, even had her kids and their friends helping out. Joe and I had several family members and Lorna, my friend from Louisiana, showed up to help. It was a great success! We made over $7,000 during our first walk and raised a ton of awareness. It was great to let the city know our programs had kept running, even though the office had shut down.

We met many new people on that first NAMI walk that were connected to NAMI as a family member or a person of lived experience. We met Marty Sexton and Tricia Wear, who appeared in costume and spoke of advocating for mental health. Only later would I realize the full extent of what these two people had walked through in life, as they have lived experience themselves. The costumes gave them courage, a facade that would mask how they really felt inside. It wasn't until days before the walk that I realized how fitting the name was: March for Mental Health. Joe had come up with it.

While I was writing my speech and was near the end of it, I wrote, "Adam wanted to call this walk 'Runs Like Crazy'. I told him that might be offensive. He said, 'My team will be called Runs Like Crazy, and that will be my Indian name from Dad's side.' (Joe had been adopted, and we discovered his birth mother was Cherokee.) 'And we will say it in German so we don't offend people. Most people probably don't speak German. That will be my name from Mom's side, Laufen Verrucht.'

"So with that, runners Run Like Crazy! And walkers March forth!" Then it hit me: Adam's birthday, March fourth! The only day of the year that gives you an instruction. So March for Mental Health it became!

After the walk, the realization that we were heading into the first holiday season without Adam hit hard. From the week he died, we kept busy, kept pushing, and kept facilitating Family Support Group and Family to Family class. Cindi turned the NAMI Facebook page over to me so I was running that, too. ReDiscover took over the Crisis Intervention Training program for First Responders in Jackson County. They held the annual C.I.T. awards at the KCPD the first year.

In the past, NAMI KC had a formal dinner when the award ceremony took place. Now, we had cookies and finger foods due to the lower budget. Joe and I received the Family Award for the second time. We had received it in 2012 before Adam took the overdose and now after he was gone in 2016. I guess they were surprised that we would stick around after the closing and the suicide. The award was bitter-sweet to us. We were being praised for all our work and for presenting at C.I.T. classes, yet we couldn't, didn't save our own son! Sitting in the row in front of me was Officer Jon Benet, who had hugged me in our home and listened and let us cry when Adam had died. Beside him sat Sergeant Greg Smith. Both of them are from Grandview P.D. I recognized them right away. Jon turned around and I said, "I remember you." He replied, "I remember you, too, Mrs. Custin. I am honored to receive the annual C.I.T. award, right alongside of you and Joe."

Wow! He said, "When we get out of these seats later, I want to give you a hug." We did, and Joe and I got to have our pictures taken with both of them. It was OUR honor! During December, we baked cookies for the Grandview P.D. and served them. The officer they sent down to get them was none other than Jon Benet! Joe and I didn't know what to do about Christmas. We and Stephanie had a rough year. Though we kept ourselves occupied, the sadness was overwhelming. I don't think a day went by without the shedding of tears. The loss of a child through death is the most unbearable, unthinkable pain. Suicide gives a whole new dimension to the grief. The would-have, could-have, should-have conversations. The self-imposed guilt. We all suffered with it. We all had health issues and eating issues. You name it, we had it. We all suffer from PTSD. Joe and Stephanie have anxiety and depression. However, somehow, Joe and I keep moving, working, and keeping busy so we don't slip and fall so deeply under the weight of our sadness that we cannot get out.

Stephanie became more and more reclusive. The toll the loss of Adam took on her was too much for her to handle. Thank God she has Marlon, her boyfriend to watch over her. We didn't want to trigger Stephanie with Christmas, nor did we want to dishonor Adam by not celebrating it. So I decorated the house as usual, crying through it all. We celebrated with Stephanie on a day in December, but not on the twenty-fifth.

That year I started something new with her to try to bring some love and joy back into her life. From Thanksgiving on, I give her a small weekly gift. She is so appreciative, and it gives me an excuse to see her.

Joe's sister Debbie invited us to Normal, Illinois, to spend Christmas in her home with her family. We had never done that before, but life in the Shultz family had changed, too, with Mom being in a nursing home. So, we accepted her invitation. We stopped in Columbia to pick up Joe's dad, Cliff, known as "Popi". We stopped by to visit Mom and then headed to Illinois.

We spent our first Christmas Eve without Adam at cousin Gary's church and headed out early Christmas morning. When we arrived, we received a wonderful surprise: it wasn't Debbie who answered the door, but Joe's brother Steve and his wife, Connie. They had driven all the way from Atlanta, Georgia, to be there with us!

We stayed in a room upstairs. A large basket sat on the dresser with goodies in it for us. The most heartwarming touch Debbie put on it was a ribbon and liner with cardinals on them and an ornament of a cardinal clipped onto the handle! She'd picked up on my love for the red birds and did this for us.

In addition to the Custins, Debbie's son Jim Ego, his wife Ashley, and their children, Sam Ego and his longtime girlfriend Misty Bradford, came over. What had been a period of dread leading up to that day was very much alleviated by the love of our Custin family. We will forever cherish that memory.

As I closed 2016, I must give thanks to my wonderful sister Ann and sister-in-law Debbie for getting me through that first year. Ann and I were born fourteen months apart, but sometimes our minds synchronize like twins. It's hard to explain, but it was like that the night Adam died, when she knew along with me what had happened.

I might mention here that we were not the only ones who felt Adam leave this world. Suzanne, my niece Jessica, and my daughter Stephanie all felt something at three in the morning, just like I did. Some couldn't identify the feeling, but all woke up shaking, scared, and thinking of Adam.

The first year after Adam died, Ann would call me at the most random times, the times I needed to talk to someone or hear from somebody the most. People always say they are a phone call away, but they don't really call, and we won't either. We don't want to burden anyone. Ann knew, though, exactly when I needed her. I would ask her how she knew, and she would say she just did.

Even though some time has passed, she still calls, knowing my heart. Debbie lost a child the day she was born, a girl named Stefanie. So she can relate to the loss of a child. She wrote me texts every Friday (the day of the week Adam died), every holiday, every significant day of the year, and even some in between. Both women were my lifelines that first year. If you love someone who has a suicide loss or the loss of a child, remember this: they won't bother you. So, please reach out and check up on them, even years down the road. On birthdays, holidays, Mother's Day, Father's Day. It will mean the world to them because even though life goes on for you, it stopped for them the day their child left this world.

That was our new normal the first year. Normal for us had been caring for our son his entire life. Without him, we were lost, so to find our new normal, we filled our time with activities, people, and business.

Chapter 8
Illnesses that Affect Us in Grief

One thing that I never realized was the domino effect that intense loss has on an individual when other people grieve. The loss doesn't necessarily have to be a death; it can be the loss of a job, a divorce, the degeneration of a living person from who they once were to who they have become (as with the mental illness dementia, Alzheimer's Disease, or cancer) All of these can create mental ailments such as anxiety, depression, and PTSD. However, even physical ailments tend to manifest. Some are brought on by the side effects of various medications, but others occur simply because our body, mind, and soul cannot seem to take another beating!

I know several members of my family deal with PTSD from trauma, along with anxiety and/or depression. Personally, I know the effects of PTSD, when certain triggers cause me to relive the horrific events of my life. I have learned to navigate it fairly well or hide it. At the same time, hiding it could possibly have triggered the physical ailments that my body has endured.

In December 2011, I had a hysterectomy. I didn't realize at the time that something that may have saved me from a future cancer growth would cause other issues. It thrust me into menopause, yet I had a doctor who didn't want to prescribe hormone therapy due to the cancer risks from my personal and family history. At the same time, she didn't offer any alternatives. So, I silently suffered.

A year later, I made an appointment with a doctor who used natural methods of hormone replacement. I had gone to see this man while my son lay unresponsive for over five weeks. I was numb and barely cared about anything at that moment; however, I had made the appointment two months prior, so I kept it. The doctor had the compassion and personality of a brick wall. He insulted me, telling me I needed to get in shape and that I was fat. (My friends laugh at this one). He was a very large man himself. I didn't speak up. I was too deep in the grief zone to absorb his abusive tone. I had already gone through years of trauma with my sick children. I was too far gone to even hear half of what he had to say.

Tests revealed that my hormones were out of whack, so I began to receive treatment through him. I continued exercising, which I have always done, but thinking all the while, What is the point? The doctor called me fat? I'm doing everything I can to move and keep my head above water and I am fat?

I was diagnosed with a thyroid disorder and took medication for that, and my weight did start to lower a bit. So, I kept seeing him. He told me that I had adrenal fatigue but didn't really explain what that meant. He treated me for six months and then took me off the treatment but never retested me to see where I was. He told me he was the only doctor in the entire Kansas City metro area who treated patients with natural therapy. I didn't question it. I just wanted to feel better.

Well-meaning people told me that I probably had depression, and if I was going to talk the talk with others, I needed to walk the walk, get the diagnosis, and get on medication. My family doctor put me on a mild antidepressant. The side effects made me feel worse, and I still had problems. I had extreme fatigue, brain fog, and joint, muscle, and nerve pain. No matter what I ate or how much I exercised, I felt bloated and more exhausted. My sleep was disrupted. I was so exhausted by bedtime that I had no problem falling asleep, but I'd wake up a few hours later and stay awake the rest of the night.

During the fall of 2015, as we were inching up on the end of our life with Adam, my doctor told me he was moving to Branson, Missouri, where his main office is located. He said he lived in an apartment in Overland Park, Kansas, part time in order to cater to his patients in KC. He told me I needed to make all future appointments in Branson, which is way too far to drive twice monthly, especially while working full time. I said I would find another doctor in the city. He laughed arrogantly at me and told me it would be impossible to find one as good as he was. He even emailed me a few times making comments like, "I know you'll be back." Or "when you decide to come around, I'll be here waiting." I knew I would never be back, not even if I had to suffer the rest of my life!

I found a doctor in Lee's Summit, Missouri, not far from where I am presently working, who practices the same kind of medicine! My old doctor had lied. There was a long list of doctors like him, doing what he does, but much more nicely! My new doctor, Malaika Woods, is the kindest, most compassionate lady. She patiently sits with me, talking me through everything in language I will understand. She has a few ladies who work with her, and they all get to know me as a person. I never feel uncomfortable.

She too put me on natural hormone therapy, but in a better way. The previous doctor had me use creams for some hormones, which were messy, and he cut into me to insert some hormones every month. Dr. Woods does everything through a painless shot twice a month and a dissolvable pill I take at night. Once again, I made my appointment during the fall, and my first one was scheduled for late December.

I almost canceled the appointment. It was five days after Adam had died, and at that moment, I didn't care about anything. As far as I was concerned, God could take me, too, so I wouldn't have to live with this pain for the rest of my life. I went anyway, like a zombie.

Dr. Woods saw through me right away and knew that something more than hormones was at stake here. She sat with me, letting me sob and vent. She was gentle and said she was sorry she couldn't erase the painful events in my life, but she was going to do all she could to make my physical life more comfortable, and hopefully the rest would fall into place.

During the spring of 2016, she too tested my adrenal glands and found that I was in a late stage of adrenal fatigue. According to AdrenalFatigue.org, it is a collection of signs and symptoms, known as a syndrome that results when the adrenal glands function below the necessary level. Most commonly associated with intense or prolonged stress, it can also arise during or after acute or chronic infections, especially infections such as influenza, bronchitis, or pneumonia.

As the name suggests, it's paramount symptom is fatigue that is not relieved by sleep but it is not a readily identifiable entity like measles or a growth at the end of your finger. You may look and act relatively normal with adrenal fatigue and may not have any obvious signs of physical illness, yet you live with a general sense of unwellness, tiredness or "gray" feelings.

People experiencing adrenal fatigue often use coffee, colas, and other stimulants to get going in the morning and to prop themselves up during the day. Adrenal fatigue can wreak havoc with your life. In the more serious cases, the activity of the adrenal glands is so diminished that you may have difficulty getting out of bed for more than a few hours a day. With each increment of reduction in adrenal function, every organ and system in your body is more profoundly affected. Changes occur in your carbohydrate, protein, fat metabolism, fluid and electrolyte balance, heart, and cardiovascular system, and even sex drive. Many other alterations take place at the biochemical and cellular levels in response to and to compensate for the decrease in adrenal hormones that occurs with adrenal fatigue. Your body does its best to make up for under functioning, but it does so at a price.

Dr. Woods explained this so thoroughly, and she treated me from April 2016 through May 2018. I did feel a bit better, but things were not perfect. Gradually, I felt the same—if not worse—being off the treatment. Was there no end in sight?

In the fall of 2017, I saw a sleep specialist and had a sleep study done. I was told I had sleep apnea, but no one followed up on the diagnosis. During the early summer of 2018, I saw an internal specialist, who referred me to another specialist, who put me on a CPAP machine. I cannot use it because I get a skin reaction to the equipment on my face! I began to doubt that diagnosis anyway. Everyone, including my doctor, said I don't fit the profile; for one reason: I'm a fairly thin person for my age.

By the way, my internal specialist and Dr. Woods said I was not fat. I was normal for my age and height! She also did a test on depression and completely ruled that out. Both women agreed that due to life circumstances, it was normal for me to experience the feelings I had.

In October 2018, I began to have intense nerve pain in my legs, along with all the other symptoms. Joe insisted on taking me to the emergency room. When I went, the doctor told me he was surprised to discover I hadn't been in before. Many people are frequent flyers to get pain medications, he told me. They investigated my history. He asked me, "You have never been in an E.R. before, have you?"

Sure I have, plenty of times, I thought. With my kids, or my husband. I don't typically do that for myself, though. Generally, I get diagnosed with something and have a surgery scheduled. I think I only went in twice, years ago—once, from food poisoning that nearly killed me, and the other from an infection due to a surgery that caused internal bleeding. I don't like taking medications, especially for pain. I just wanted a diagnosis and a cure, once and for all!

Through testing and a follow up with my internal specialist, I learned that somewhere along the line, I had contracted Human Parvovirus, which is more common to people who work closely with young children. I also had Epstein Barr in my blood. I went on with my life and took some pain medication and steroids to end the current suffering.

By April 2019, I had almost had enough of it! I was falling asleep at random times, in addition to all the other symptoms I'd had for at least seven years! I told Joe I felt like I was constantly walking through mud and dying a slow death. I decided to do some research on my own. I researched all my various diagnoses, including Rheumatoid Arthritis, which I had been diagnosed with in my thirties. When I hit on Epstein Barr, I found every symptom and every illness I have dealt with related to that one virus: chronic fatigue, sleep disorders, pain, etc.
I bought a book on it and followed its advice step by step. Within four days, my mental fog was gone. I actually had been beginning to think I had early onset Alzheimer's. My father had been diagnosed with it around my age but died at 81.

I am now sleeping better. Not perfect, but better. I don't fall asleep during random times. I rarely experience joint pain unless I eat something I find I have an allergy to. With this virus, a person can develop allergies to foods and environmental substances, and I am finding out through the process of elimination what these are. There are a few things I cannot eat or drink anymore, but I feel so much better! I take a lot of natural supplements to detox my organs, which have been affected by this virus. Doing this gave me the energy to get through the day. That is why I finally finished *Adam's Contract with God.* To me this was a miracle!

I still get sleepy at some point during the day, but a nap usually gets me back on track. When I get to feeling sluggish again, I know it is probably because I ate foods that caused it, and I do a reset. It is a battle I will probably have the rest of my life because I love sweets and dairy, for example, but since adrenal fatigue came my way, they don't do me any favors.

When I feel sluggish, I do a reset on my way of eating and usually get back on track. I put this information in here because many people going through what I am going through, are feeling the same way. I am on a Facebook page, Families Dealing With Suicide, the Next Chapter, and see a lot of this. Adrenal Fatigue, one of my diagnoses, is connected to Epstein Barr, too. My doctor told me that I can control a lot of what goes on with my choices in life, but I have no control over what happens to me. It can be devastating on the human body.

Epstein Barr is not uncommon and will always show up in my blood; however, it can be more extreme in some people (like me) than others. When environmental and emotional events occur, it can make it worse. I say, if you are in my situation and feel like this, get tested and then take measures to feel better. It will not just go away on its own, and we have enough to deal with handling our grief without it messing with us as well! I have learned through my own process in illness with grief and difficult times, that other illnesses can get worse: anxiety, depression, heart disease, hypertension, and high blood sugar, to name a few.

I recently learned that there is an illness known as "Broken

Heart Syndrome", a temporary heart condition that occurs after an intense physical or emotional event. It is a type of non-ischemic cardiomyopathy in which there is a sudden temporary enlargement of the heart muscles. A person can feel like they are having a heart attack with sudden chest pain.

Not everyone who is grieving in the manner that we are has Epstein Barr. Not everyone has Broken Heart Syndrome, but if you talk to most people like the ones I am connected to on parent loss websites, we all seem to have common symptoms, and yes, we become ill. Grief creates stress in our bodies; when we grieve so deeply, we feel out of control and disoriented. Many of us feel extreme exhaustion. Simple daily tasks become a big chore. Thinking clearly is a thing of the past. Our judgment and ability to problem solve is impaired. We feel alone and disconnected from the world; isolated. Much of that comes from feeling like we cannot grieve openly or talk about our loss in front of people, even those close to us. Holding it all inside is very unhealthy. Intense grief can trigger anxiety attacks, depression and the desire to abuse illicit or prescription substances to fight the pain. All these stressers can lead to a weakened immune system.

Before Adam's death, I prided myself on how strong my immune system was. I had worked with children for many years and faced many illnesses from the children and others that surrounded me. But after Adam died, I caught anything the wind blew my way.

What can help? Support groups in your city for suicide or any kind of loss or online support groups. Some people do better in person, while it is easier for others to be online where no one sees them. I chose to go online, not because I can't face people, but because I am actually so busy with work and volunteering, that it is easier for me to go online whenever it is convenient. I also recommend seeing a counselor if you feel so out of control that you need help to get out of bed, cope with the loss, or need an unbiased person to hear you. My therapy has been on-line support, helping others through NAMI, and helping other families who are dealing with suicide loss.

Chapter 9
Survivor of Suicide

I am a survivor of suicide. What does that mean? I've never made an attempt on my own life. I always thought of suicide survivors to be those who attempted suicide and somehow survived. Adam was a suicide survivor many times over. How can I be one, too? I know we are all considered survivors when someone dies. It is listed in every obituary. It has always been a strange concept to me because it was someone else's suffering that I survived. I didn't go through what that person did, be it cancer, a heart attack, or suicide. Yet, when I think about it, with the word "suicide" attached to "survivor", it really does make sense, especially if you were really close to that person.

Suicide is a death like no other. That person who took their own life chose to die. You were powerless to make them stay. Your love wasn't enough. You didn't save them! Somehow you must have been guilty of something to MAKE them want to die, right? So many thoughts swirl around in the mind of a suicide survivor. The emotions are not like those accompanying other deaths—those deaths you can somehow blame on something else. However, suicide has to be some-one's fault, and how can you blame the one who died and cannot defend themselves? After going through the loss and incredible grief and witnessing others' reactions through survivor support groups, it occurs to me that "survivor" is a very appropriate term for us.

Why? Because you go through such intense emotions and guilt along with that loss (which is often of a young person), that you begin seeing no reason to keep living yourself. Many follow the trend. It can cycle like that through families. It is sad and frightening. Personally, I never wanted to kill myself, but I must admit to going through a phase of not really caring if God decided to take me suddenly or if I never woke up again. To wake up would be to relive every emotion and agony all over again when I realized my son was gone forever. My Adam was not coming back.

It takes great strength for a mother or a father to keep on going without their beloved child. So, yes, I AM a survivor. I lived through it and you can, too! I decided to be proactive and find a way to live out Adam's legacy in a positive way. To continue support groups for others and give them hope. To keep NAMI alive in our city somehow.

As time went on, I discovered so many ways to live Adam's legacy and to give meaning to his life. That is why I am a survivor of suicide! Surviving suicide is NOT staying in bed all day feeling sorry for myself. It would be so easy to do that. Instead, I choose to get up, get that first cup of blessed coffee, say my prayers for the day, and talk to my son, because I believe he can hear me. Then I get up and go to work like everyone else. I give thanks for what I have and the people in my life now, and yes, I also give thanks for my boy and the joy he gave me, and for the fact that he no longer feels the pain and shame of this world. I think of ways I can help someone else.

Yes, this is how I survive. It isn't easy some days. Sometimes, even now, I want to wallow in my sadness. I want to feel envious of those who have what I will never have: a living son, grandchildren through my children, a college graduation, a wedding. Well, maybe I will have that. I pray for it, but I know there are no guarantees in life, so I have to learn to accept and appreciate what I do have. I might hurt if I am at a wedding or if a new baby is born, when I witness the joy of others, but at the same time, I am thankful for what they have because

I would never wish this sadness on another human being, ever! I am a suicide survivor and this is my life now.

Chapter 10
Year Two

The year 2017 was a very significant year. It was Year Two following our loss. In January, our niece Addie, my youngest brother Martin's daughter, asked us to come to a musical she was in. She was twelve at the time, and her brother Alex was almost sixteen. Martin's children are sailing along smoothly through life, and I pray they always will. They are the light of Martin and Angie's lives and with good reason. Though they make mistakes as all kids do, they are a light. At least in our family, they are. Alex and Addie chose to be with us when Adam was taken off life support in 2012 at such a young age. They are ever present in Joe's and my life to this day. We are grateful for them and for their health! We enjoyed the musical and were honored to be guests. Though, it saddens us when we realize that our children (or, we) never had these milestone moments, like prom, or weddings, or college, we are overjoyed to see them succeed.

In February, we began to plan for the second walk. Tyler Sharpe was working on his Master's Degree but still worked on sponsorship for us behind the scenes. I am so thankful to him for his support and friendship.

I was still in the process of figuring out what was wrong with my health during this time. I was on a website called "Nextdoor" that our neighborhood is a part of, checking out posts. I didn't realize it incorporated around nine neighborhoods, some from Grandview, and some from Belton. We are only a few minutes away from Belton. A lady named Krissy Revert posted something about natural products she was selling with Melaleuca and how dangerous many of our cleaning products are. I had often wondered how many of our illnesses, including mental illness, could be wiped out if people stopped consuming processed foods, GMOs, hormones, and such. I also wondered if the chemicals in our cleaning products could be harming our health.

I wrote to Krissy and said I was interested in buying some of her products. I have allergic reactions to cleaning products, and their smells make me sick, so it was worth a try. I could have just bought some product from her, but if you joined a membership, you received big discounts, so I did. I didn't intend to sell it, but I do buy their products monthly, as they have made a difference.

This part of the story is not really about Melaleuca, but it was the factor that introduced me to Krissy, who became a friend for life from that day forward—one of the most important links in our chain in life. I didn't know it the day we first talked, but she would forever change my life, Joe's life, and so many others for the better.

Krissy is about seventeen years my junior. She and I talked for a long time during our first conversation. It quickly evolved from a discussion about Melaleuca and how chemicals affect us to me sharing my thoughts on how they affect people with mental illness. She agreed with my opinions.

We shared stories about our lives. Krissy is married to a man named Mike, who endured a very tragic childhood. He was so badly abused, one might wonder how he even walks though this world. He suffers from Schizoaffective Disorder, a mental disorder in which a person experiences a combination of Schizophrenia and mood disorder symptoms. Genetic factors and changes in the brain function are responsible for the condition. Symptoms include delusions, hallucinations and depression. Treatment includes psychotherapy and medication. In his earlier years, Mike was diagnosed as bipolar, also known as manic-depressive illness. It is a mental disorder caused by structural and functional changes in the brain or changes in genes.

Affected individuals experience episodes of depression and episodes of mania. Bipolar disorder lasts for a lifetime, with treatment aiming at managing the symptoms by psychotherapy and medication. When someone with this illness becomes depressed, they may feel sad or hopeless and lose interest or pleasure in most activities. When their mood shifts to mania or hypomania (a case less extreme than mania), they may feel euphoric, full of energy, or unusually irritable. These mood swings can affect sleep, energy, activity, judgment, behavior, and the ability to think clearly, according to the Mayo Clinic.

A few years before I met Krissy, Mike had been in a terrible motorcycle accident. Prior to the accident, he had run his own business and was able to live a full life with medication. After the accident, life changed for both Mike and Krissy. Mike's symptoms were very difficult to manage with either therapy or medication. He is a wonderful man, who has had so much taken from him. It didn't seem fair to me.

Mike went through many, many shock therapy sessions and high doses of medications that only made things worse. Finally, a doctor put a stop to these sessions. Things seemed to improve for a while, but as it seems to go in life, these things were short lived. Mike is now in the fight for his life on a daily basis. So is Krissy! They have two kids: a daughter who is in her late teens and a son who is around fifteen. They are not without their scars, either. I have said it before, mental illness affects an entire family, not just one member of it.

Shortly after I had first met Krissy, she was attending my family support group at Research Psychiatric Hospital. She is bright and articulate, and she offers so much to the conversation. It wasn't long before

I realized what a gem I had found in Krissy. Not only did she stand in as my co-chair when Tyler couldn't make it, but she is very energetic and faithfully throws herself into causes she feels passionate about. She became my rock—the person I could count on for anything!

The dreaded month of March rolled around. March is so bitter-sweet for Joe and me. We were married on March 4. Adam was born on our second anniversary. While he was alive, we celebrated him on that day, and we chose a different day to celebrate our anniversary. Now the day was all ours, is all ours, but in our hearts it is still Adam's. So, we celebrate our love each year, knowing Adam is in our hearts always.
In March 2017, Adam gave me a gift. A memory I had forgotten popped up on my Facebook news feed. Somehow it gave all that guilt in me a reprieve. He had sent this message to me on his last birthday:

Heidi, Momma, this is for you. For keeping me sane all these years. I could've swallowed the bullet, but there's you that keeps me round, helps my thoughts stay sound. If you weren't the same person you've always been, under any circumstance my life may have been lost. This song goes out to you for keeping your heart, mind and body full of everything it is. I'll never get tired of listening to you, as you have proved throughout my life you will never get tired of listening to what is in my heart. I love you dearly Mom.

Your favorite son, Adam.

Greg Laswell, who sang the song "And Then You", told me how appreciative Adam was to have me as his mom, in spite of the thoughts, dreams and love that let him down in his life. It gave me more credit than I felt I deserved some times. Still, I will treasure the song as long as I live.

In early April, Krissy began pressing us to go to her church. She had been at it for weeks. We were Catholic while she attended a non-denominational church in Belton. That was NOT us. At the same time, the only time we went to church was in Columbia with Popi. That was becoming a pretty regular thing because he was all alone without Mimi, and it gave us a chance to visit Mom in the nursing home, too. Krissy wanted us to meet her pastor, Chris Pinion. She said he was interested in bringing mental health awareness into his church.

Clever lady, that Krissy. She knew it was our passion and said she would get us in touch with him. Helping others was something we couldn't pass up.

So we arranged to meet him at a Starbucks in Belton, one of Chris' favorite meeting places. It seems he loves his coffee! I wore my NAMI badge to look more professional. When Joe and I showed up, he was seated at an outside table talking to another pastor who was passing through. It didn't take long to realize how well known he was in that town. People even drove by honking and waving at him!

Pastor Chris Pinion has a very magnetic personality. People like him immediately. His enthusiasm for whatever he is passionate about in contagious. He is in his late forties and has a tall, stocky build, wavy brown hair, and twinkling blue eyes. He pretty much hooked us the moment he said hello. He didn't just shake our hands, he enveloped us in a warm hug. He said, "I already know you are going to be a big part of LifeQuest Church!"

I wasn't sure what he meant by that. Did he want us to bring NAMI into his church, telling our story? Or did he think we would become members of his church?

Joe went inside to get a cup of coffee. I said, "Look, Pastor Chris. I need to tell you something while Joe is inside. I was raised Protestant, so LifeQuest is probably not a far reach from my roots." (It was, actually! The Methodist church was far more traditional.) "You have to know something about Joe, though. He was raised Catholic. He is a 'cradle Catholic'. We have both been Catholics together for about twenty-five years."

"Are you practicing now?" he asked.

"Well, sort of. When we go to Columbia, we go with his dad. We just haven't found the right church to attend since we came back to Missouri."

"How long have you been back?"

"Um…eight years."

"Like I said, you are going to be a great part of LifeQuest Church! Hey, there's Joe! C'mon over, Joe. Let's talk about having you and Heidi tell your story to our church and bring in NAMI to support people who need it there."

The next Sunday, we decided to go to church at LifeQuest with Krissy. We figured it would make Chris and her happy. We stood in the middle of the back row, feeling a bit out of place. First a worship team played and sang music—really upbeat music; nothing we were used to in either the Methodist or Catholic churches we'd attended. People were singing loudly and dancing around, and it seemed that everyone was genuinely having a great time. We went a second time in April. We were a bit more relaxed, but like the first time, we bolted before anyone could ask us any questions.

As we were preparing for our upcoming talk at LifeQuest, Stephanie quit her job after nine years. The effects of the trauma she had endured in her life had taken its toll on her—from her childhood illnesses, to her rape at the age of fourteen, to the six years of abuse she'd suffered at her boyfriend's hand, watching her brother wither away and die, twice. She became ill herself. She was diagnosed with PTSD, anxiety, and depression.

Once again, we are grateful that she has Marlon in her life to love her along with us. Marlon has a son who was nine at the time they met. He lived with his mother but now came and stayed with them more and more. By August 2017, he moved in permanently. While at first it gave her focus, it became difficult for her over time. He had experienced some trauma of his own and acted out with uncontrollable fits of anger. These fits were usually directed at peers his age, but Marlon still had to deal with other angry parents, teachers, and school administrators.

Throughout it all, we continued to provide a support group, Family to Family classes, and Crisis Intervention Trainings around the city. In April, we were invited to do our first C.I.T. in Sedalia, a town in rural Missouri. I attended the first one alone, as Joe had a work obligation. However, I was so excited about it that my enthusiasm infected him. He has accompanied me ever since.

When held in a city environment, C.I.T. is forty hours of intense training during a single week. In rural counties, there is not enough manpower to do this all week long, so they have a five week, one day per week training. C.I.T. is badly needed everywhere, but there are far fewer resources for the mentally ill in rural counties. We are thrilled to open up new possibilities for people we may not otherwise be able to reach.

We always say that mental illness does not discriminate. It doesn't care what your socioeconomic status, race, or creed is. It doesn't care whether you live in the city or the country. As Joe says, it is an insidious disease that creeps in at will and destroys individuals and their families. We travel about four times annually to serve C.I.T. in these counties. It is very rewarding, and we have had a great response to question-and-answer sessions following our presentation.

Also in that April, our nephew Christopher got married. We all stayed in cabins at the Buffalo Outdoor Center in Arkansas, near the Buffalo River. The plan was to go canoeing and have the wedding in one of the larger cabins. It rained a lot and the river was too high to float on, so we did some hiking and lots of visiting with all the guests. It was a pleasant weekend in every aspect.

Having said that, it was the first wedding we had attended since Adam had died, and it was for Chris, who I loved like a son. I felt like I had bravely approached the wedding weekend and thought I had a great attitude for it. With a loss like we had suffered, I learned that no matter how hard you prepare for something coming, you can't possibly know what your emotional state is going to be. Like the first Christmas without Adam, I was expecting that day to be the worst ever, but it ended up being peaceful, and we were surrounded by great love and support.

I happily joined Ann in decorating the wedding couple's cabin and setting up for dinner. I was having a great time the whole day. I even managed to make it through the wedding itself with only the kind of tears one would normally cry at a wedding.

However, the celebration that night at the cabin was different, and my reaction was totally unexpected to me. We were all stuffed in there, body to body. People were toasting the bride and groom. Ann stood up and gave a toast. She talked about how happy she was for them, how she had gained a daughter and a grandchild and other things. It was a perfectly delivered speech.

All of a sudden, my brain did a flip, and all I could think of was what I would never have now. I had tears in my eyes and was fighting to keep them from spilling out. I got a lesson in grief that night, that I was not to grieve in front of other people. I was to keep it to myself and try to get over it.

A person I dearly love had a bit too much to drink that night (I forgive this person; I only tell this to give an illustration of what we go through). Said person marched across the room, looked me in the eye, and said, "You don't get to do that here. Just stop it now!" That really helped me control the tears! I quickly escaped to the back of a stairway leading to a loft above. The bathroom door was on one side of me, the master bedroom on the other. It was a perfect place to hide. I was shaking uncontrollably. I felt humiliated and ashamed. I was to be the ruin of everyone else's good time, but most really didn't even notice. As I shook under those stairs, a hand reached between them, taking mine.

My nephew, Alex Shultz, was sitting on those stairs. He was sixteen at the time. "You will never be alone," he said, as if he could read my mind! "I love you and I will always be a part of your life. You will be in my future children's lives, too. I will never leave you."

A moment later, little sister Addie took my other hand from between the stairs and said she would never leave me either. True to their word, these two often reach out to me with such compassion and love. I love them so much.

A couple of adults noticed me behind the stairs and said I didn't have to hide, that my feelings were valid, and that they supported me. Thank you, Brad and Jessica Burbridge, Alex, Addie, and Kristina for how you treated me that night. Because of you, I was able to reel it in and enjoy the rest of the night. We all put on glow-in-the-dark necklaces and danced around outside, being goofy. The day hadn't been ruined!

On the weekend prior to Memorial Day, Joe and I made a presentation to LifeQuest Church. The stage was set up comfortably with large, soft chairs and a table to put our water on. We were given microphones. Both of us were nervous. We had done this many times, but this was a totally different kind of venue. Pastor Chris assisted the presentation with an interview format, guiding us along gently. We finished only to have to do it a second time for the next service!

Even though Joe and I are familiar with the statistics, that one person in four will be diagnosed with a mental illness during their lifetime, we still were not prepared for the onslaught of people who greeted us in the main lobby following our sessions! We stood separately on either side of the main entry room. We each had a line of people with many questions or stories of their own to share with us. Each and every one of these people had a huge impact on both of us.

By the time we reached our car, we were both emotionally exhausted (events like C.I.T.s can do this to us). We have learned that it may take a day or more to recover after opening the wounds over and over again, but the rewards make it worth it. We both agreed that this church needed NAMI support systems put in place, so we had work to do. We talked about the people who had stood out to us.

I told Joe that two men in particular had drawn me in. Their names rhymed, I joked. Zach and Mac. Zach Gardoski is a singer with the LifeQuest worship team. He had just moved to Kansas City at that time. His kindness and love for others immediately melted me, seeping into my soul. I knew that first day we met that we would be great friends.

He had lost a close friend to suicide, so he could feel my pain. Zach has beautiful blue eyes and wild curly hair like mine, and his voice is so soothing that I feel like I am always safe near him. He is a gentle giant.

The other person, Mac McDonald, is about a year and a half older than me. He is a tall, slender black man who can light up a room with his smile. Joe and I both said similar things about him after meeting him. I said, "I looked up and him, and he smiled at me with a kind, gentle smile. He had an aura about him I cannot explain, but it was beautiful. He didn't relate a similar story or life, but I felt incredible love flowing from this man. This peace. I felt like I had known him my entire life." Joe said the same thing. Little did we know that day that he would play a huge role in our lives, and everything we sensed about him was true. Like us, he had been through some horrible things in his life, and he was hurting like we were, just in a different way.

During the remainder of May and into July, we alternated between attending LifeQuest Church and going to Columbia to see Mom and take Popi to church at the Newman Center on Mizzou campus. We both agreed that we found LifeQuest to be our religious home, but we felt we couldn't tell Popi for fear of breaking his heart that we didn't attend a Catholic Church in Kansas City. He had turned eighty-nine in June. There was no sense in saying anything.

During the summer of 2017, many people were recruited to create new classes and support groups for NAMI-Greater Kansas City. From our church, Krissy Revert and Sue Teagarden trained as Family Support Group Facilitators. Mike Revert and Shawn Teagarden trained as Peer Support Group Facilitators. Amanda Cousins, Sarah Gregg, and Linda Schoor became Family to Family teachers.

From among my NAMI friends, Marty Sexton and Trisha Wear trained that summer as Peer Support. (They have since gone on to become certified in many other programs, including Ending the Silence, a NAMI program designed for going into schools and talking with youth about mental health and suicide prevention.) Pam Kreutzer and Holly Behrens trained for both Family to Family and Family Support. It was thrilling to see how much people around our city cared about NAMI and its services to the greater Kansas City area. Even without an office to call our home, volunteers from around the city rallied to keep it going and growing, helping people in need. Missouri NAMI continued to have our back and encourage us along the way.

June was a very good month for Joe and me. We continued to forge new relationships in our church, which got us out and doing things besides volunteering—things that would help us advance on our path to healing. We got closer to Krissy and Mike, and Mac McDonald, and met with Terry and Becky Luna. These would form the core group of people who would get us out into the world again. These people hadn't known us while Adam was alive or had even known him, but they gave us the great compassion that we needed. They let us say his name and talk about him anytime we needed to. We all need people like this in our lives.

At the end of June, we celebrated Popi's 89th birthday in Columbia with the Custin and Shultz families. Sadly, it would be his last. A couple of weeks later in July, Popi called me, sounding very disoriented. He left a message on my phone saying he was in trouble and couldn't move. Joe called him but didn't get an answer. He then called Tiger Place, the facility where he lived, to alert the staff.

We went there immediately. Popi was in his bed alone. The nurse had come in to check his blood sugar, and since it was okay, she had gone! We called an ambulance. We had tried to feed him soup, but he kept falling from a sitting position, and the spoon kept slipping out of his mouth. We had a week with Popi in the hospital, feeling like he was getting better at times, then worse. A week following his admittance, we lost Popi. It was a very sad time for the Custin family. He was the last of Joe's parents and a most amazing leader of the family. I was blessed to have him as my father-in-law, and all who knew him were likewise blessed.

Popi (Cliff) was a retiree of State Farm Insurance. He had risen to the top, serving as a Regional Vice President. He was kind, thoughtful, and wise; he loved God and his country. He was an Army veteran and proudly wore his cap to let everyone know it.

It brought many conversations with strangers his way. We loved him so much, and even though he would thank us for spending so much time with him during the two-and-a-half years after Adam's death, he was the one who needed to be thanked. He gave us HIS time. He gave us purpose. When he left us, LifeQuest stepped in. We are grateful we were able to spend his last week with him. Every one of his kids and spouses—Custins and Shultzes—had the opportunity to say good-bye to him and to tell him how much we loved him, and he got to tell us the same.

At LifeQuest we met many people, both through our NAMI work and through attendance. We learned of so many stories of mental illness and suicide like ours. Angela Bollinger is a sweet lady, a few years younger than myself, who had a story eerily similar to ours. Her daughter Cassidy had survived after being declared brain dead from an overdose and lived to tell the story. Angela is also a survivor of stage four cancer, but since her remission, her cancer has returned. However, she is a fighter, like her daughter. I love them both and have had the opportunity to get to know them, both in the church and outside of it. Krissy Revert, our great buddy, has fought many battles, along with her husband and children. In August 2017, she lost her brother Joey to suicide.

Zach, the man I met after our initial presentation to the church, has become a great friend and prayer warrior for our church and us. We have had the pleasure of his company in our home and at a Hill-song concert, and dining out with the worship team. Mac, although he hasn't had issues with drugs or in dealing with mental illness, is part of a group called Save One Life, an organization started by Mike and Mindy Horton from LifeQuest, who both battled addiction at one time in their lives and now support others who are in recovery. Mac posts a daily prayer and an uplifting message on their Facebook page.

Linda Schoor, now a great friend, met her birth family (siblings) and discovered that both of her birth parents had died by suicide. Linda now understands where her depression and anxiety come from, as many times it is genetic.

Dawn Farrill, whom I cherish deeply, has a very loving soul and a dreamy face, and is so kind. She has shared with me the day she was on the brink of suicide and her return to life. She told me the day Joe and I spoke, she had wanted to end it all, but we changed her mind! I love her!

Mike Revert has shared with us his long history of child abuse and the chain reaction of events that happened since then including a Bipolar diagnosis. I love his honesty. This man and his wife are the real deal, and with them, we have made friends for life.

Terry and Becky Luna have various family members who struggle on both sides of their family. They have taken on many young people into their home who have struggled, nurtured them, and helped them get back on their feet. Terry, also known as "Papa T", has played a big role in our lives and in Lil' Man's life, too. These two got Joe and I out to Saturday night karaoke at the VFW in Lee's Summit, Missouri, where we met even more people we now call friends. Terry and Becky, as well as Terry's sons, Ryan, Mac and Joe, all sing on Saturday nights. It is very relaxing and enjoyable, something we needed in our lives. We hadn't socialized like that since we were with the old gang in Broken Arrow, Oklahoma, back in 2008.

Amanda Cousin's mother has Schizophrenia, and now Amanda teaches Family to Family and understands her mother's illness better.

Our own pastor, Chris Pinion, bravely came out and told of mental illness in his family. Why do I call him brave? Many pastors will not talk about this subject, for fear of losing members of their church or their own credibility. In LifeQuest church, our pastor opened so many doors BECAUSE he opened up.

Lloyd and Avis Curphey, dear friends from a connect group we now attend through the church, have shared so much of themselves with me. Avis had a sister who had Schizophrenia. Lloyd has been diagnosed as Bipolar. They are both amazing and inspiring people who have been through so much trial and pain yet light the way for others in such a beautiful way.

My neighbor, Mylissa Russell, also attends LifeQuest. She has gone through hell and back during her life, struggling with depression and attempting suicide multiple times. She is another beacon of light who leads others down a path toward brighter days. I have also had the opportunity of knowing her son, Jacob Kalianov, a delightful young man whom I wish Adam had met. He has faced and conquered many battles, and I feel they could have been a great support for one another. Jerry and Robbin Loftin, two of my dearest friends and part of my NAMI walk team in 2017 and 2018, have struggled with their kids, mental illness, and their own battles. They have inspired me with their strength through some tough times. They also lost a nephew to suicide since we have known them.

Recently, I met a young lady named Kristen Haak, who lives with Schizophrenia and has frustrations similar to the ones Adam had. She is amazing. She attended the women's retreat with LifeQuest church in May 2021 and handled the group like a champion!

Hailey Revert, Mike and Krissy's daughter, came on board in 2017 with NAMI walks. She designs all of our T-shirts and is a great artist inspired by her own battles with depression.

Jeff Kroenlein, who attends LifeQuest and is our Thrivent agent, has helped to get funds raised for NAMI and our endeavors. He has become a valuable and trusted friend to both Joe and me.

Two couples who approached us early on and made us feel very welcome at LifeQuest are Dan and Deb Braun and Don and Dana Bass. Both couples support our NAMI functions and are part of our Connect group with Pastor Matt and Penny Mills. We joined Matt and Penny's connect group in July 2017, shortly after we joined the church. Krissy Revert pulled us in there, too. Through our weekly meetings, we have met so many wonderful people who have enriched our lives so much.

That month we volunteered for LifeQuest's fireworks tent. Just this event alone changed our lives and the lives of many of our family members. We got to know the Lunas even better. Krissy and Mike, along with the Lunas, basically ran the whole tent. I really know nothing about fireworks, but I can pick up on someone stealing, and it was our job to notify Terry Luna or one of his safety patrol people in the event we witnessed this happening. Terry, although only five foot six and sixty years of age, would chase these folks down. Some were huge, but he was tough. He had led a hard life in the past and turned his life around five or so years before we met him. I would never have guessed that he had run with gangs and such. They say dynamite comes in small packages, and that was Terry. He had a mischievous spirit, and we could see it in his twinkling blue eyes.

There was an older woman who came into the fireworks tent with her family. She was around sixty years old, her daughter was around thirty-five, and her young grandkids were with them. The two women had their little ones fill their baskets with small, inexpensive fireworks while they shoved larger, more expensive ones inside their dresses! They paid for the cheap fireworks and left. Terry caught wind of this and chased them down, demanding to see what they had stolen.

He called the police, and the women were arrested. The police later called and asked Terry if he wanted to press charges. He said he wouldn't if the grandmother apologized. She heard him on the other end of the phone and began cussing him out. So Terry pressed charges. Our safety patrol included Leon Schoor (Linda's husband), Don Bass, and Mac McDonald, all of whom were former police officers.

My sister Kristina was newly divorced at this time and feeling alone. She lived in Columbia, Missouri, at my mom's house, which was two hours away. I told her to come join us. We were working at the tent. She was not big on the idea because she had to drive back home that night and work the next day. Plus, it was raining and would continue to rain late into the evening. But she showed up. She wanted to stay in the car, but I encouraged her to come out and meet the wonderful new folks in our lives. She did, and met Terry, Becky, and Krissy.

Terry had a pile of fireworks stacked in the middle of the aisle he called a "cake", large ones on the bottom, smaller ones on top. He priced the bundle as a deal. Kristina was interested in seeing a firework box on the shelf and tripped over the cake, knocking it down.

Terry came over to help her. She had a huge purse and jokingly told him it had been her plan to knock them down, then squat down to "pick them up" but actually scoop them into her suitcase of a purse. We laughed and Terry said he'd come after her if she took anything.

We went to the other side of the tent, and I introduced her to Mac. They hit it off immediately. Joe and I had been spending time with this jewel of a man, and I thought at the moment how nice it would be if Kristina and Mac became an item. They had both been through two rough marriages and divorces. Looking at them, I wondered, could this work?

While she was talking to Mac, Krissy thought it would be funny to stuff long sparklers and other noticeable fireworks in Kristina's large purse. Then both of us called out to Terry: we had another theft on our hands. Kristina had no idea they were there. Terry stumbled over with a limp due to previous cancer he had beaten and landed a smack right on her butt. She thought it was Joe, since our family does this "good game" thing and turned around to "get him". In shock she saw it was Terry, a man she had just met. We all just about died laughing. Welcome to LifeQuest Church, Kristina. No perfect people allowed.

Mac and Terry both fit right into our family as we are all clowns, loving a good joke and a laugh. Mac ended up getting Kristina's phone number by a mistake in communication. Both talked about how their kids went to Hickman High School, so they exchanged numbers to see if their kids knew each other. Later on, they learned that one went to Hickman Mills in Kansas City, and the other went to Hickman in Columbia. No matter, from that day on, they began messaging each other and talking for hours on the phone. It didn't take long before they were an item.

Mac, the man we felt had a halo over his head the day we met, would now be a part of our family. Because of their union and traveling back and forth from KC to Columbia and vice versa, we got to see Kristina nearly every weekend. She became part of our karaoke family and part-time church member. While in Columbia, she attended our cousin Gary's church, Revolution. When Kristina and I were younger, our parents moved to Topeka, Kansas, for two years with our little brothers. She was sixteen and I was nineteen. She ran away from Topeka straight to me. I was living in our parents' Columbia house paying rent and renting two rooms to help out. Kristina wanted to finish high school at Hickman, so she lived with me. She went to school, worked a job, and was no problem. We became pretty close. Over the years, when I lived in Oklahoma and she went through two marriages, things changed a bit. For twenty years, we only saw each other on holidays and at special family events. However, now we had the chance to renew our friendship, as well as our sisterhood.

She and Mac have both been an integral part of our healing. They brought laughter back into our home. Joe and Mac are now like brothers. Mac tells total strangers they are identical twins. The bright ones laugh, but some say, "Really?" as if the light bulb died. Mac is over six feet tall, and Joe is around five foot seven. Mac is black. Joe is, as he puts it, "fish belly" white.

When someone says, "Really?" Mac often replies, "Yeah, Momma loved him better than me. She kept me in the oven longer until I burned to a crisp." Still, the blank stare! Both have lost their hair, though, and both have a chipped front tooth and numerous scars on their heads from accidents and such in the same places! Both have skinny legs. If you ask them on any given day what color their underwear is, they will peel back the waistband of their pants to reveal the same color. They have similar tastes in clothing. Both are intelligent and can carry on a conversation on various subjects. We really do have a good time together. We do have our laughs but can also speak of our pain (all of us) without judgment or shame.

Mac is a big prayer warrior and will pray for and with us, too. In August 2017, Sadie started what they call Preschool Prep, a program for two-year-olds. She was two-and-a-half that June, so she was more verbal than many of the children who had just turned two.

The Petersons have become more and more like family to me over the years, and I have developed close relationships with both Nick and Sadie. I took Sadie to Preschool Prep on Tuesdays and Thursdays from 9-12. When I picked her up, she was quiet and sat all prim and proper on a carpet waiting for me. Sadie, by nature is NOT quiet at all. She has a loud, booming, playful voice and spirit. She wears dresses and leggings (her choice) every day and looks like a little lady, when in reality, she is tomboyish during outside play and girlish (think tea parties, dolls and dress up) during inside play.

She is delightful, is full of mischief, loves animals, especially dogs, is quick to laugh, and rarely cries (even during falls). She is the perfect little girl, if you ask me, with all the character traits one would find fun, amusing, and sweet all rolled into one little girl. Her mischievous side came out the first day of school. It being the first day of school, she'd had it in her mind that her mother would be picking her up. We all told her otherwise, but her stubborn side came into play that day. She decided if she played her cards right, Mom would indeed come and get her.

Now Nick had been going to that church for Preschool and Pre-K the previous two years, and I knew the director and his teachers. They were all on the main floor, but Preschool Prep was in the basement where we rarely saw the other staff. Sadie's teachers were new to me, too. Sadie and I are very close, and we loved to hang around together, so I figured she would be happy to see me. However, when she has her mind set against something, it is not happening! Of course, she was two years old, too. I went to pick her up that first day. There was a low wall between the classroom and the parents, so people could clearly see everyone. I know she saw me, but she never made eye contact. I was impressed, because I thought that not only was she was following rules and waiting to be called by the teacher, but she was not freaking out or crying when she saw her person like ninety-nine percent of them were. But nope. Those were not the reasons. She had decided that her mom was picking her up, and she wasn't going with me if she had anything to say about it!

So, I checked her out on the sign in/out sheet. I smiled at her. "I am here to pick up Sadie Peterson. I am Heidi Custin. I am on the pickup list." Suddenly, Sadie grabbed her teacher's leg and looked up at her (a lady she had just met) with pleading eyes and said, "I do not know that lady!" All of a sudden, I was suspect. Why in the world did she do that? Luckily for me, the director just happened to be strolling along that floor and said, "Hey, Heidi! How's it going?" Relief swept over me. I had just known the cops would be called, and I would be taken away.

When I asked Sadie why she did that, she simply told me that she figured her mom would come and get her if she said she didn't know me. At two years of age! Smart kid. Mom and I both talked to her about how wrong that was, and she never did it again. As the first weeks of school passed, the teachers could see for themselves how much she loved me by the way she ran into my arms with hugs and kisses every day thereafter. She still remained still on that carpet and didn't move until called—very obedient.

I didn't see her mingle with other children for the longest time. I asked her every day if she had made any new friends. One day about three weeks into the school year, she finally gave me an answer: "I play with Adam," she said.

I couldn't remember seeing a child by the name of Adam on the roster. I looked the next time, and there was no Adam or anyone with a name close to that. I asked her what Adam looked like. Who she described was my Adam as a toddler, with blond hair and big blue eyes. A while after that, we were at my house playing, and she saw a photo album on the coffee table. Leafing through it, she came upon a picture of Adam at two years of age. "There's my friend, Adam," she stated as if it was a matter of fact.

I was confused. How could this be? She was only one year old when he died, and he had brown hair as an adult. She had never seen a picture of him as a young boy before. Did Adam appear to her as a toddler, like he did in so many of my dreams? Could it be possible? She leafed further through the photo album and pointed out an adult picture of Adam. "This is Adam, too." she said. I was dumbfounded.

We spent our summer moving from dinners and snow cones with Tim and Laurie from next door to hanging out with our newfound friends from church at volunteer activities and karaoke, to meeting even more people at the VFW. Joe and I began volunteering to watch the young children of the single moms during their Bible study time. We continued to make more and more connections.

Many opportunities to help others came into play in 2017. Joe and I were regularly called in for C.I.T. training in Jackson County, Missouri, and now the rural presentations were catching fire! More people wanted to jump in to raise money for the NAMI cause. A lady who lost her husband to suicide organized a motorcycle ride to raise money.

Joe and I shared our story in Family to Family classes for NAMI, a class designed for family members of those living with mental illness. I found that keeping busy kept me moving and kept my mind occupied. Sharing my story made people realize that Adam was a real person with real feelings. He had an illness. He lived with Schizophrenia, but he wasn't Schizophrenia. It didn't define who he was. It made me realize we all need to tell our stories. We shouldn't feel shame in that any more than if we had a diagnosis of arthritis, cancer, or diabetes. The more we share, the more people will listen, and the more they listen, the sooner change will come!

Sadly, in August, our dear friend Krissy lost her brother Joey to suicide. He stepped in front of a train. Now we needed to be there for Krissy as she had been there for us. We were so thankful that she too had NAMI in her life to help her get through it.

September rolled around. The annual SASS-Mo-Kan Walk happened. We participated in that and will continue to do so in the future. It won't matter how many times we do it; hearing our son's name read from the list of suicide victims is alarming to hear every single time. We are amazed at how many participants stand with us, so many with loved ones lost to suicide, and we know we have to end this cycle some day!

We joined our friends Clay and Allie Hugill and Bob and Becky Beers, and this time around, we walked for Clayton, Adam, and Joey. The same day we participated in our first Crazy Love with our church. Crazy Love is a day where we go out to various chosen places or to people who are in need and help them for a day. It was a very rewarding experience. All in all, September 10, 2017, was an emotional but rewarding day!

On September 25, Stephanie turned 28. Every time she has a birthday, I can't help but think about how old Adam would have been, yet he was stuck at 24. He should have been 26!

On September 30, we had our second NAMI-GKC walk! So many people still believed our city was done with NAMI. How awesome it was to let them know how much we had grown in the year since our office closed down. Many new groups had been formed, as well as more facilitators of all our groups and teachers. It felt very good!

During the month of October, another miracle happened in our family. Lil' Man (Marlon Jr.) had come to live with Stephanie and Marlon Sr. He was playing outside their apartment building with some other children. One child threw a ball up onto the third-floor balcony. Lil' Man told the kids he could scale that building and retrieve the ball. While he made it to the balcony, he lost his grip and fell. The ground below was rocky, and he landed on his back and was temporarily knocked unconscious.

A friend went to call 911. Suddenly, Lil' Man stood up and walked upstairs to get his dad. He told him what had happened, and he and Stephanie took him to Children's Mercy Hospital.

His back was compressed, and he had some strain in his neck area. He wore a back and neck brace for a time, but he survived! He is alive! If you saw the place he fell, you couldn't help but wonder why he isn't dead or at least paralyzed. That night, Marlon Sr. drove Stephanie home from the hospital so she could rest. It was around two in the morning. She walked into the apartment and across the room she saw Adam there, standing sideways. She said, "Adam!" and suddenly he was right in front of her, and then he was gone.

We know in our hearts that Adam saved that little boy that day. He lightened his fall and came to let Stephanie know he was going to be okay.

The holiday months were approaching once again, in our second year without Adam. Joe and I talked about it, and in spite of all the activity and all our new friends, it somehow felt more difficult to face than year one.

I think this was partly because during the first year of loss, everyone rallied around us, and quite frankly we were still in shock. The second year brings panic: our loved one is really gone. We realize it fully then.

As more time passes, will we forget his face, his voice? Will he disappear from our lives altogether? This thought is pure agony.

Joe added another activity to his week. He began tutoring Mike and Krissy's son, Mikey, who was struggling in eighth grade. Boy, did that bring back memories. Eighth grade had been a nightmare in our household, with puberty and all the changes it brought. It was when the switch was first flipped in Adam's brain. Of course, Joe wanted to help Mikey and hopefully prevent this from happening to another person we love. We got to know him very well. He loved my cooking but ran from my hugs. He is funny and bright. It strengthened our growing bond with the Reverts.

During December, we kept our calendar full to distract ourselves. Joe was teaching Family to Family, along with everything else he was doing. We had a December C.I.T. in Jackson County. Our State Farm friends, Brad, Tracy, Tony, and Karen, took us out for dinner. Another group from State Farm invited Joe and me to a Christmas music program with their agency team. That was enjoyable, yet painful at the same time. Some of those songs brought back the pain.

Joe and I took our pastor Chris and his wife Linda out to dinner. Our bond was getting stronger with the church, and Chris had huge ideas for helping people from our church and others with mental health. It gave me ideas for NAMI walk number three for 2018. We would post a challenge to schools and churches around the city to sign up for the walk. The group with the most volunteers would receive $500 for their organization. We were pumped!

We spent a quiet Christmas with Stephanie and the Marlons, senior and junior. Lil' Man was becoming one of our own. My Christmas present was a surprise trip to Jamaica for the remainder of our holidays! Just Joe and me. We went to a little resort and stayed there the entire time, hanging out at the beach and enjoying each other's company. It was just what the doctor ordered. Once again, alone, we shared happy and sad memories. We laughed and we cried. It was what was necessary to face the beginning of year three. In 2017, I had learned that it was okay to cry. I also learned it was okay to laugh again without guilt because I would never hear Adam laugh again.

Adam had brought our family to God in 2012, but I felt disappointed and hurt that God would have let this happen to us again and take Adam away for good. In 2017, I let God back into to my life. I opened my heart again to letting some healing happen. Life wasn't perfect, and to our family, it never will be, but we have so many people in our lives to help us navigate through it: our lovely family, our NAMI family, our wonderful neighbors, and most certainly our LifeQuest family.

Pastor Chris had it backwards when he said we would play a big role at LifeQuest. LifeQuest and the people there played a big role in our world and lives, transforming our hearts and our souls.

Chapter 11
The Unwanted Attention

After Adam came out of his coma in 2013, my cousin Pastor Gary Powell interviewed our family on Adam's near-death experience. When we attended his church that Easter Sunday, he presented the video of us ("Adam Custin Miracle" on YouTube). We attended with Adam. My mother warned me to stay close to him because people might want to touch him, thinking something spiritual might rub off on them. She said they might become obsessed. I was very protective, and people did touch him, but he came out unscathed.

In 2017, after we gave our presentation at LifeQuest church, I experienced what my mother warned me about. It was subtle at first but gradually developed into something disturbing for me. When I entered the church for our presentation, I carried in boxes of NAMI information.

The first person I encountered was "Mandy". She was standing near the information desk, so I figured she worked or volunteered there. I asked her if she knew where I should put all my boxes. She happily took the boxes from me and said she would handle it from there. Following the presentation, she was among the people waiting in line to talk to us. She told me that her best friend had taken her life, and was seemingly very empathetic towards us.

Of course, I reached out to her; that's what I do. That was how she hooked me. She requested me as a friend on Facebook, as did many other people I had spoken with at the church, and of course I accepted, oblivious to the fact that was step two of her plan. Shortly after that, she asked if she could call me "Mom". I told her that I have a daughter and she has a mom, so I declined. She asked me if she could call me "Grandma" since, as she put it, "You will never have grandchildren of your own." I was taken aback, as that was hurtful and inappropriate. I told her I wasn't old enough to be her grandmother; I am about sixteen years her senior. It didn't take long to tire of her messages. She'd just met me, and already she was professing her love for me dozens of times daily. I noticed over time that she wasn't quite right, to put it kindly. I put up with her antics because I didn't want to hurt her feelings.

She seemed to show up everywhere—at events I attended, at restaurants where we ate, at church services. She was even in our Connections group. It became very uncomfortable. As I became acquainted with others in the church, I received warnings from several people. I was told to block her and that I was not the first person she had stalked. Even though I was losing sleep over it and becoming frustrated beyond my limits, I still couldn't do it.

Then someone showed me Mandy's Facebook profile on her phone. Her featured photo was MY picture! She had told her Facebook friends that we were best friends from twenty years ago and that we had recently found each other again. According to her, I had lived in Oklahoma twenty years ago! At that moment, I knew that the woman Mandy had told me about, who had taken her own life, was not really Mandy's best friend, but someone she had stalked.

She forced herself into pictures taken of me with other people, holding onto me roughly so I couldn't get away. At a NAMI walk, when my friend Elizabeth Wilson was taking pictures of the event, she maneuvered herself into several pictures with my family and friends. Once Elizabeth understood what was happening, she deleted those and took new ones. Mandy sent me messages of her "singing", if you can call it that. Songs about grieving. It was horrible. It was torture. It sounded like a gaggle of geese squawking!

My husband didn't notice all this at first, and agreed to give her rides home from Connections. Her mother has cancer and is elderly, but Mandy lives with her and doesn't drive due to her disabilities. So she warmed up to Joe, and his kind heart went out to her. She wrote me letters all through church services and bought me things. They were small things, yet she'd go on and on about how much she had spent. "It cost me a pretty penny, I tell you! A whole dollar!" she told me one time.

Once on the way to her mother's home, she said, "Why don't you just take me to Byars Road so I can go home with you?" I got chills because she had never been to our house, nor had she ever been given our address. I told Joe that she was not as innocent as she came across. A friend told me she was at home one time and received a call from Mandy asking her to go hang out with her. She told Mandy she was busy. "Oh, no you're not! I am sitting outside your house and I can see you!"

Chilling! How she talked someone into driving her to do these things is beyond me! People came forward to tell me that this "sweet" lady would become violent if you turned her away and had even attacked individuals in the church. Now I was afraid to tell her to go away.

Another friend from the church who had lost a child had been the recipient of Mandy's stalking before I came along. She had encountered Mandy at church one day, and Mandy had a picture of her son drawn on her arm. She proudly told my friend she was going to have it tattooed there! My friend told her that was not happening! Mandy went on to create a Facebook page in the child's name! I decided to check my own name on Facebook. I was pretty sure I was the only Heidi Custin on there, my surname being a dying name and my first name being so unusual. To my surprise, there was another page in my name! Luckily I had caught it before she'd had a chance to do anything with it. I messaged "Heidi Custin" and let her have it. Nothing else was ever done to that page. Then she apologized (after telling me it wasn't her who did it). Why would someone apologize if they did nothing wrong?

One night at the VFW in Lee's Summit, while hanging out with friends and listening to karaoke, Mandy began sending me Facebook messages. I was annoyed. My friend Terry Luna grabbed my phone and blocked her from my Facebook. So she began texting me, begging me to add her back on Facebook.

One of our pastors called for a meeting between Mandy, her mother, Joe, and me. She promised that all activity would cease. It did not. On our way taking her home from Connections one night, she said excitedly, "I have to read you what I wrote. It's a true story. On Christmas Eve, 2015, I woke up suddenly at three a.m. I felt Adam Custin's soul leave his body, and I knew I had to meet his mother and be a part of her life. What do you think?"

She also said she showed people pictures of him (from my Facebook page) and told people that he was her boyfriend! I was in the front passenger seat and Joe was driving. Mandy was in the back seat. It was dark. I stared angrily looking forward. I was so distraught I couldn't speak. Joe dropped her off and said, "Wow."

I lost it. "The first part of the words in that story are MINE! That is MY story! MY life! She can never ride with us again! I am done!" I blocked her from my phone this time, ending all possible communication. She tried to get to me at church but was sent away by others every time. Two very loyal friends, Becky Luna and Robbin Loftin, kept a close eye on all her movements. She sent me notes in church begging me to add her on Facebook or unblock her on my phone. She said she was sorry. I told her it had happened one too many times; bad behavior has consequences. If she was going to act like a child, she would be handled accordingly.

Eventually, she started stalking someone else at the church and was asked to leave permanently. She still shows up occasionally at random outdoor events, and once she approached me in Walmart after I had published *Adam's Contract With God,* telling me I needed to do her a favor and get her a copy. I told her she had to buy one somewhere else. Sisters Debbie and Kristina were with me, and I thought those Mama Bears were going to tear her a new one! She has tried to message me on Facebook messenger with, "I love you! I miss you!" and I ignore it. I've heard that she is now attending another church. I feel their pain! Many people had left the church before we attended because of her. So sad. This is an example of what my mother warned me about with Adam, and I was thankful he didn't have to experience that!

Chapter 12
2018

Joe and I became very busy in 2018. Planning for our third NAMI walk was in progress, and that year it was set for May, earlier than in previous years. Krissy and I had more people on board with us than ever before. Isabelle, our faithful friend from NAMI, the Loftins, Jerry and Robbin and Mike Revert, worked especially hard to make this one count. We decided to write as many churches and schools as we possibly could around the city to draw interest for the walk. Mental health awareness is so important in both places, especially with rising suicide rates around the country.

My team worked so hard, yet didn't drum up much interest from other churches. But wow, did LifeQuest step up in a big way! We had a contest to see who could come up with the biggest walking team, and that organization would receive a $500 check from an anonymous donor. Some called us to meet with us. Krissy and I talked to several groups from schools, detention centers for troubled youths, and churches. Many of them were excited about the idea, yet when the time came to walk, few showed up.

We did meet a lovely couple from another church in Belton, Pastor Damon and his wife Beverly Brewington, who jumped in with both feet and haven't stopped! They have a small church, Believers in Glory in Jesus Christ Church. Beverly is ahead of the game and runs a support group in her church for families of the mentally ill. She has speakers from C.I.T. officers to psychologists to people with lived experience in recovery, and more come to her group. We have partnered with her in her walks and NAMI walks. She invited Krissy and me as speakers to her group. She is working hard on legislative issues and trying to reduce stigma in the black community. I have learned so much from her on double stigma among minorities, and see it in my own family and with friends, as much of my family and friends are of color. All of them agree that it is taboo to talk about in their culture. I applaud the Brewingtons and their mission.

Beverly inspired me to provide pictures when I do public speaking, as she calls it "Putting a face to the disease". I have had so much positive feedback ever since I changed the way I did things. It does bring our stories to life!

In January, I reconnected with my dear friend, Sarah Boyce from Shawnee. She was the one who took over for me with my nanny child, Tyler Wilkens, when I fled to Adam in the coma. She and I decided to make monthly dates for breakfast or lunch. She has encouraged me on this book journey and remains a great support.

We had a cancer scare in January from Joe's brother, Steve. His wife Connie is a breast cancer survivor herself, but what were the chances he would have the same diagnosis? Joe and I flew to Atlanta to be there with them. Lots of prayer chains were sent around. He had a malignancy. After surgery and removal of the cancer, the doctor said it was benign. Miracle or mistake on the doctor's part? I don't know, but I have witnessed too much in this life not to lean on the side of another miracle!

In late March, we had a helicopter Easter egg drop for the kids. A few thousand people attended. It was crazy. Our church does amazing things! I was handing out snow cones as fast as we could make them. Others were handing out hot dogs, popcorn, and cotton candy. There were games and jump houses. Wow! If only we could get a response like that for NAMI!

In April, Joe joined the church band. At this point, we were doing something nearly every single night, and it was wearing us both out. On alternate Mondays, we went to my M&M group in Pleasant Hill, or Family to Family class for Joe. Tuesdays, it was Connect group at LifeQuest. Wednesdays we alternated walk planning and watching little ones for the single mom's group. Thursdays were for NAMI support group and band rehearsal for Joe at the church. These were just the evening activities, following long work days for both of us. Then add C.I.T., and other events and health fairs, writing when I could, running a Facebook Page for NAMI-GKC, and attending both church services every Sunday for me to serve and Joe to play guitar or drums with the band. While we loved doing these things and all the people involved with them, it was wearing us down. I still had an undefined illness and slept only four to six hours a night.

We didn't commit to anything on Friday nights unless Mac and Kristina came to stay. This helped to promote a calm and relaxing environment because we didn't have to go anywhere or do anything, and Saturday nights were mostly reserved for karaoke at the VFW in Lee's Summit. We love it, but it does go late into the evening, which makes for a short night before Sunday morning rolls around. We talked about ways we could cut back and do a reset. We decided to cut back on the Wednesday night gig with the kids. We love them, but that is exhausting physically.

I went to my first women's retreat in April (it was the first one for LifeQuest, too) and it was wonderful. Imagine fifty-plus women not bickering, just caring for one another! A week later came the third March for Mental Health! LifeQuest won the $500 and gave it back to NAMI. The donor wrote LifeQuest a second check!

That same year, LifeQuest celebrated its first fifteen years, and we had a night of worship where people gave testimonies as to what the church meant to them. Shortly before the celebration, Joe said, "Oh, yeah. You and I are speakers tonight. Guess I forgot to tell you." I was panicking a little! He said he hadn't planned anything either, so we both winged it. You couldn't see past the first row because of the bright lights, but someone said afterwards, "Wow, you two were the only ones who got a standing ovation." I didn't even know, but as those words were said, Krissy passed by and said, "Stage whores!" Oh, wow. We all cracked up laughing. Krissy is great! She is that one person who can say anything and get away with it, even in church!

May was a difficult month for Joe, me, and our entire family. My mother passed away. I was blessed to be at her side the week before she passed and the day she left. She told me the day before that she was looking forward to going home. She had been in a nursing home since Adam's funeral services, over three years earlier. She told me she was going to plant a garden in the backyard and have fresh tomatoes like the old days. She spoke of all the meals she was going to cook, like Swiss steak and green pea soup, but without flour-based dumplings, because "I don't want to kill Kristina!" (she has Celiac). She asked for a chocolate malt, and Joe promptly ran out to get one. People questioned why she wanted that since she had stopped eating by that time. "Because she wants it," he said. She held it like a baby holding a sippy cup on her side and sipped two-thirds of it down before falling asleep.

My siblings Lisa, Martin, and Kristina were there, along with Mac and Joe. My mother's last moments were not easy, and I was looking her in the face and beginning to panic. Ann and Jimmy were present via speaker phone, and Ann, who is very protective of me, yelled, "Get her out of there!" I refused, and the others didn't understand why she had said that. I knew why, however, and that's all that mattered. She had held me when Adam was taken off life support, and she was holding me from a distance that day.

Three days before Mom died, we had to run to KC so I could get a vaccination. Our last pet, Nellie, had passed away that day, at the age of sixteen. She'd had cancer. She had been our last animal connection to Adam. Joe commented on how our lives had changed so drastically in very short order. "We are orphans now. We are empty nesters; no kids, no pets." These are two things we had our whole lives together—our parents and our animals.

During the summer, we took on Lil' Man and Aunt Debbie's dog Rusty (formerly Popi's). They both helped keep us busy and fill the hole left by all the losses.

During this time, Terry Luna's cancer returned, and our friend Angela from church was dealing with cancer, too. Terry and Becky continued with the fireworks tent that summer. Joe, Lil' Man and I volunteered most days. Other times Lil' Man accompanied me while I took Angela to appointments and brought her food. I got to know her very well that summer. Not only did her daughter have the same miracle as Adam had, but we both ran child care businesses during the same years.

On June 9, Terry turned sixty-one. Along with the Lunas, Mac, and Kristina, we met Ann and Victor in St. Louis for an outdoor concert to celebrate. It was a very hot day, but we had a great time. Terry sat in his lawn chair mostly, as his energy was low. We also spent time in Columbia, where my cousin Gary prayed for Terry. My Columbia family was with us. Between Jackson County and Rural C.I.T. trainings, we were going to one or the other every month. I love how many people have been reached through this program!

In July, our church had an outdoor baptism at Longview Lake, and Joe and I decided to do it again, by our own choice this time since we'd both been baptized as babies as is the Catholic tradition. They literally dunked us Baptist-style!

Following that, Lil' Man went home to prepare for the school year. The family I work for generously provided him with new shoes and glasses for school. He had spent a lot of time with us over the summer, and loved Nick and Sadie. He even spent Fourth of July with them. How blessed I am to have this wonderful family in my life.

In the first weekend of August, Joe and I took Rusty to Hannibal, Missouri, to meet Debbie. I spent a lot of time there as a child, as my great-grandmother Shultz had lived there, and we'd had Thanksgiving family reunions there every year until she passed away. Joe had never experienced Hannibal before, and it was a good halfway point for Debbie. We stayed the night.

The next morning, Joe and I both woke up around 4 a.m. We started talking and laughing about something. I can't remember what, but suddenly we were both quiet for a good ten minutes. Then I heard a calm, gentle man's voice say, "Stay close to God."

"What did you say?" I asked.

"Stay close to God," the voice repeated.

"Was that you, Joe?"

"What are you talking about?" he replied.

"Did you just say, 'Stay close to God,' twice?"

"No."

However, I had clearly heard it, twice. Now what was I to do with that information, and what exactly did it mean? I consulted Joe, Mac, Zach, and other friends, including Camille and Tina from church. They are like spiritual leaders to me. The responses I received from these people were similar: You are on the right path. Stay on track. Keep doing what you are doing. God is looking favorably on you. The strange thing is that I've never feel like I measure up to any of these people in God's eyes. When people look to me for guidance, I sometimes feel like a deer in the headlights, overwhelmed. However, hearing something like this made me realize how important my faith was, and that I definitely needed to stay on track!

August through October were crazy busy months. We had taken Wednesday off our plate, and Joe had backed off teaching Family to Family for a while, yet many things were added to our plates. Pastor Chris began with a vision of educating pastors and chaplains as first responders in the field of mental health.

We met Ayme Trefethen and fell in love with her and her daughter, Olivia! Ayme is involved with NAMI in many ways and is trained on almost everything they have to offer. She has lived experience and brings so much knowledge to the table, both professionally and personally. She met with us and our pastor and planned out a mental health first aid course and QPR (question, persuade, and refer) for the pastors and chaplains. Joe and I attended, yet I got sick and didn't complete it, so it is on the agenda in the future! I did complete QPR, however.

On August 11, we went to see Matt Maher, who lives just down the road from us with a ton of friends from church.

We began to get close to Jeff Kroenlein, who worked for Thrivent Financial, and began doing business with him, in addition to developing a great friendship with him. He was with us at the concert, and that day we began to plan a benefit for Terry and Becky Luna to help with their mounting medical bills since Terry could no longer work. His doctors said he was terminal but could live for twenty years with the proper treatment.

We participated in Beverly Brewington's walk for mental health. Many churches in Belton banded with her to raise awareness. They asked me to speak at one of their luncheons and for Joe and me to hold a NAMI booth. We were honored and amazed at how the black community in Belton was so proactive in this fight! So proud to be a part of it, and they welcomed us like family.

On August 25, we had a spaghetti dinner at the VFW for the Lunas. I cooked spaghetti sauce all week prior. I cooked so much, I was dreaming about it! The fundraiser was a great success. We raised enough money to pay off the medical bills and more!

On September 9, we participated in our fourth SASS walk.

On September 23, we participated in Crazy Love with our church again. We may have been backing off on Mondays and Wednesday a bit, but we were more than making up for it every weekend. The next weekend was the pastor/chaplain training we had planned for in August.

October rolled around. Jennifer Burnett, the lady in New Franklin who had made the quilt out of Adam's shirts for Joe and me, was ready to give them to us. She was having a walk/run in Columbia to benefit the school her daughter attended and to honor her daughter Kelsi by raising awareness for Cornelia De Lange Syndrome. The event was called the Spunky Monkey. Her daughter had loved sock monkeys, and they'd named it for her.

Joe, Martin, Ann, and I showed up for the walk, and Jennifer presented us with the quilts she'd made. In addition, she gave Joe a framed quilted piece of an art piece Adam had made many years before entitled "DAD". We hugged each other and cried together. What an amazing gift, and lady—so selfless in her own loss.

On the following weekend, Mike and Mindy Horton had a dart

tournament event to benefit NAMI-GKC. Joe and I attended and spoke there. Krissy, Terry, and Becky came, too. Terry was getting weaker, and we began to question this "maybe twenty years" thing. However, Terry remained upbeat and hopeful, looking forward to a new grand-daughter to be born in April, and a cruise he had planned for March 2019, on which Joe and I were renewing our vows after thirty years of marriage.

In October, everything was catching up with me health-wise. I was having episodes of narcolepsy and joint pain, and I felt foggy in my brain and very disoriented. I had a sleeping disorder. I told Joe, "It feels like I am walking through mud and not getting anywhere. I feel like I am dying a slow death and nothing can stop it." For three days and nights, I had the most debilitating nerve pain in my legs. I could barely walk.

That month I canceled my plans for NAMI walk number four. I felt like I had let so many people down, but I had to slow my life down and figure this out before it killed me. I added Trisha Wear to the NAMI-GKC Facebook page to relieve me of that duty. She was phe-nomenal. She handed the situations with people with lived experience and passed-on family members, which are way fewer, to me. She too became overwhelmed in 2019 because she volunteers over the top, too. Gabriel Sparks and Brian Reser, both of whom I have had the pleasure to meet, are now taking care of that for me. I had to back out on some Monday meetings with the M&M ladies, and some Tuesday nights as well. For me, I was down to Tuesdays (sometimes) and Thursdays, hoping for some healing.

In early November, our church started a health and job fair called H20, which has been pretty successful. Now about four times a year, they set up for this. They give a "hand up" to help people in need, rather than a "hand out". I set up a NAMI table and get to visit with people who come in, often right off the streets. It is easygoing and laid back. Food is served, too. "Grandma" Deana Flemming and Krissy Revert run it. In 2021, it became so successful that we began to do it once a month.

Once again, the holidays were approaching. We wondered what we would we do that year to "celebrate". Becky Luna has a large family, much like the Shultzes had at one time. She invited Joe and me to join them. I was nervous, but wow, we were treated just like family. Joe and Harold (one of her brothers) played guitars, and many people sang. Becky and Terry both sing karaoke, so it was like a big band of players and singers. It was very nice and fun. Ryan, Terry's son, spent time with me while they played. Joe and I were getting closer to the entire Luna clan. Kelsey, Olivia and Ryan's daughter, calls me "Nana Heidi", as will Mia when she gets older.

On December 8, Joe, Mac, Kristina, and I attended "Sampson in Branson" at the Sight and Sound Theatre. It was a Thrivent group from church featuring Jeff Kroenlein and his wife Krissy, and Mike, and a few others. Thrivent is a wonderful non-profit money management organization. What is exciting about Thrivent is their Action Teams, which give back to the community. When you are a part of Thrivent, you have $500 to spend annually (divided into two) on a fundraiser or cause to help someone else. It is a big part of our church and has helped fund many events, including our Sing Out the Stigma for NAMI, Save One Life (planned for April of 2019), H20, and Christmas shopping for those in need. These are just a few of the many things they fund. Jeff sets up events for us to get to know each other throughout the year, too. It is always a great time.

I received a call from Kathy Mahoney (from our church) in early December. She told me she participates in a program called Paws for Autism. She foster-cares dogs who are trained to provide comfort care to people with special needs. There was a dog named Bentley, who was two and a half who needed a permanent home, a "change of careers".

I wasn't sure what that entailed, but she told us she thought of us first as he had worked with families of suicide before. She knew we had lost our last pet. Joe and I were undecided about getting a new one and starting over, but the more Kathy talked about Bentley, the more we liked the idea. We decided to meet him. "What kind of dog is he?" I asked. She said he was a standard poodle. Joe and I cracked up laughing, wondering what we would do with a fru-fru dog. Then we saw a picture of this magnificent, beautiful black-and-white dog, and we knew he would be ours.

Terri Wible, who works with Paws for Autism, delivered Bentley the day after our Branson show. We were so excited. Mac and Kristina were there, and Stephanie and the Marlons came a bit later. Bentley was very tall! He was so majestic looking and sat so properly that we cracked up. We asked Terri why he had to have a "change of careers". "Let's just say he needs lots of patience and love," she replied. Well okay! We sure had a lot of that to give.

Stephanie looked him in the eyes and he loved on her. She cried. I am thankful for that bond as she takes care of him when we travel as she did all our other pets. She had two chihuahua mixes who are very protective of her. One is older and blind. He ran toward Bentley and went right past him! The other sat on her shoulder and bared his teeth, growling at him. She says when he is at her place, he just rolls them around with his paw like toys. Hilarious.

The first night Bentley was in our house, Joe and I were in bed, when suddenly he appeared on the bed between us. He didn't jump; he just seemed to levitate. Light as a feather for his tall frame, he weighs a mere fifty-seven pounds.

We learned more about Bentley as the days, weeks, and months went on. He would take a hold of one's wrist when they came through the front door and lead them wherever he wanted them to go. Becky Luna jokes that he won't let her leave. She heads for the door, and he repeatedly brings her back to the couch. I had to put a stop to him doing that to me, as it hurt my small wrist bones!

I taught him to grab a favorite toy. He brought with him one known as "the puppicino", and he now has a blue stuffed puppy he adores that Nick picked out for him. When I or Kristina arrive, he goes to get one of those or one that looks like a dead possum and prances around like a show dog. Other than that, fru-fru does not describe him in the least! He has a deep bark, which is scary if you don't know him. If you watch television (which is rare for us) and an animal appears on the screen, he goes crazy, leaping and barking at the screen!

If you do not put a lead on him while walking him, he will bark at rabbits, deer, and other people on the trail. With a lead, he is peaceful and calm. He snuggles and thinks he is a lap dog. He is smart and knows many commands. He is very sweet. We love him to death and are so glad we made the choice to keep him. However, we see clearly why he might ruffle the feathers of someone with special needs when he gets rambunctious.

On December 15, the worship team invited Joe and me to dinner and a Christmas lights tour of KC in a limousine. It almost seemed like our people were conspiring to keep us busy during December. Well, they did a good job of it.

The next weekend, we had our family Christmas dinner at our house with Stephanie, the Marlons, and Camille and Zach from church, who happened to be alone that Christmas. It was a great evening with all. Tough as it is for Stephanie, she bonded with both of them. Camille and Zach are very special to us. I can't explain it, but they have this deep spirituality that goes beyond what many people see or feel. Stephanie tuned right into that and told me later that they both had good "auras".

My niece and nephew, Brittney and Byron, were stationed in Wichita Falls, Texas, for a few years before moving back to California in 2019. They invited us to join their family along with Mac and Kristina for Christmas. I warned her that I might have meltdowns, and she said that was to be expected. They would be there for us.

Christmas was very busy, with many people around. We didn't have time to be sad. I went to bed every evening feeling very loved. I went to bed early because I was exhausted, and a storm had caused them to lose their electrical power. The lights suddenly came on when I was asleep. I heard someone say from the living room, "Aw, there's Adam." I got up to see what was going on and found them watching a video of their wedding. Sure enough, there was Adam, as a teenager. All in all, the holidays went beautifully, and we talked to Adam in the dark and wished him a Heavenly Merry Christmas.

Chapter 13
Stephanie

As I have told the story of Adam's life, I have thrown in bits and pieces of Stephanie's. I talked about her illnesses and abuse. I want to let you know her a bit more, too. Stephanie is our firstborn child. She was the most outgoing little girl, very determined to have things her way. I loved that spirit in her, even though she challenged me along the way. She was a tough little girl from around aged three to six. I thought I had my work cut out for me. She did not like having to share her mommy with a group of other children, which I understand, but I wish she would have known from the start that no one could replace my little girl, ever.

Then we started our Girl Scout troop, and Steph and I did many fun things together. All her good friends were in our troop. We cooked, camped, danced, and did all sorts of girly things. Steph was a good friend to many, and often her group would fight over her. She loved life. She loved her family. She especially loved her little brother. They were a team.

I witnessed so many things go wrong in Stephie's world but always felt she came through fiercely. She almost died a few times, not by her own choice: from the tick bite at six, from Type 1 Diabetes rearing its ugly head at ten, from complications of diabetes mixed with flu, and from being in danger of an abusive man who beat her badly. Yet, she still kept going. I thought she was so strong. Losing her precious brother Adam was the straw that broke the camel's back. It may not have taken her life literally, but it stole her life as it was. It took the determined, tough little girl right out of her. All of the pain and suffering Stephanie had endured built up in her over the years. The repeated trauma caused very complicated symptoms of PTSD, anxiety, and depression.

She recently quit her job and now stays at home. She is trying to piece her life back together with the help of Marlon and us. One step at a time. Even with all that being said, something amazing has come out of this experience with Stephanie. As much as we pushed going to church on our kids in their youth, she fought against believing there was anything beyond this world for so long. However, after Adam's near-death experience, she began to change, and quite frankly, I think she understands more than the average person. Her spirituality is so beautiful. She sees and feels things most people don't. She sees Adam. She sees a little sister she never met, who died before she was born. She sees other spirits.

She once sat in church and told me things about people she didn't know, and she was spot on! She knows where her brother is and where we will all be one day. She sends me beautiful messages of hope and love, not quotes from another, but her own thoughts. Stephanie loves animals and all creatures. She loves deeply and mourns deeply, too. She has come to the same conclusion her dad and I both agree upon—that life really is all about love and caring for one another. She is love. She judges no one. She is a beautiful creature.

She once told me that if we hate another, judge, or disrespect, it is like handing them poison to drink; only it poisons the person giving it instead. If you choose to discriminate against another person, then YOU are the one who is suffering. At the end of the day, if you have hate in your heart, you will never be happy. She is so right. She is our love, created in love. She is our one and only, our girl. Our daughter.

I dedicate this story to Stephanie Elizabeth Custin and her Daddy, Joe. I pray she finds strength to fight for her own life and finds a way to live for Adam. He would want that more than anything. Stephanie also told me this, "Being successful has nothing to do with the type of job you have, the amount of money in your bank account, or the type of expensive things you own. Being successful is overcoming your battles, surviving your journey, and gaining experience. When you are at the point of being able to share your collected wisdom with the world, then you are at the highest point of success there is."

During 2020, when the pandemic hit, it was a relief to Stephanie not to feel pressure to leave her home. We did not see her much but found out later that she was working on herself and healing through online support groups. She is doing much better, and we asked Stephanie and her partner Marlon to join us in the Dominican Republic for my sister Kristina's wedding to Mac in June 2021. It was her first vacation with us since Adam came home from his coma in 2013!

Chapter 14
Choosing Joy

J.D. Salinger (author of *The Catcher In the Rye*) wrote that the most singular difference between happiness and joy is that happiness is a solid and joy a liquid. I think of happiness as something we feel when good or exciting things happen in our lives. It can be a vacation we are excited about, spending money, a new car or house, or a delicious dessert. It is something that is achieved by acquiring material things or experiences. The feeling is expressed more outwardly. It is a temporary feeling. I wonder how many people truly feel happiness. Joy is a more internal feeling, more spiritual, more satisfying. It is being thankful, having concern for others, and being grateful. For us, it is finding these things in the wake of tragedy and grief.

Often, joy comes with self-sacrifice, and being selfless can bring on joy. I won't ever find happiness in having biological grandchildren, yet I can find joy in witnessing others do it. I can find peace inside with joy. Joe and I get joy from serving others, be it at church or with NAMI. Helping others less fortunate or in crisis and seeing a positive outcome brings joy.

I believe that only those who can look beyond their own problems and can see beyond the immediate gratifications in life, helping others and seeing the beauty in what we are given, can feel true joy. I try to concentrate every morning during my prayers on what I am thankful for without focusing on the loss and sadness in my life, and there I find joy. The things I now find my joy in are seeing a newborn baby, holding him or her, and soaking in the fact that this is a true miracle in life. I find joy in our worship songs in church. They sometimes move me to tears, but there is joy in that, too. I find joy in holding Joe's hand or in his warm, loving hugs and knowing how safe and protected I feel in his arms.

I feel joy knowing my family, daughter, siblings, and theirs are okay or happy, even if it means they have what I don't. I feel intense joy every time I hear of the successes of the children I helped to raise in Oklahoma. It makes me feel that maybe I did something right. I feel joy watching the deer and cardinals in my back yard, and bunnies hopping on the trail. I feel joy on a walk through nature. I find joy in Bentley snuggling up to me. I find joy when I spend time with my daughter, and when I hear her laugh. I find joy in fellowship with friends and family.

Joy is God-given. The night Adam died, he changed his profile picture on Facebook from a picture of himself to a picture of a smiley face with the words, "Be Happy" written underneath. Most of us who belong to the loss-of-a-child club or the suicide-survivor club have this sense that we will never be happy again. I still feel this way myself. To be happy gives me feelings of guilt, as if it is undeserved somehow.

Feelings of joy, on the other hand, I am finding more and more in my journey. It is what I choose and how I choose to live my life. It is how I feel helping others. Somehow it is like me telling Adam from this place to his in Heaven, "See, I do love you and I continue to love you by doing the things I do." In turn, I find my pieces of joy.

I cannot feel guilt, as my joy comes from the benefit of others. It truly is living the legacy of Adam. Like Stephanie told me the other day, "The hand you were dealt has no significance, but the way you deal with your hand has all the significance."

Chapter 15
2019

The year 2019 had its ups and downs. In January, our dear friend, Terry Luna, passed away. I was facilitating a NAMI support group meeting when I received the call. He wanted Joe, Mac, Kristina, and me. His son Ryan was a wreck and needed Joe. I fled, driving as fast as I could. Joe was practicing with the band at LifeQuest. I stopped there first and picked him up, calling Kristina on the phone. She left Columbia immediately, hoping and praying she would reach him in time to say good-bye.

Terry lay on his hospital bed in their living room with family and dear friends around him. Pastor Chris came and prayed with all of us. Terry told us he had seen Jesus earlier that day, and he was ready to go meet him. I sat beside him when it was my turn and gently hugged him. He had become so fragile I feared I would cause him pain. He said not to worry about that. He told me he was excited because he would get to meet Adam soon, and he would take care of him. They would both be watching over me.

Joe had found a great male friend in Terry. He was upset but tried to be strong for Ryan and Becky. Becky had us worried because she seemed too strong. She was worrying more about her kids and grandkids and everyone else than herself. Maybe it was the nurse in her. I have watched her during the months since. And yes, she has her breaking points just like everyone else. Kristina had a two-hour drive, and when she got there, Terry said, "It's about damn time." We got a chuckle out of that in spite of our sadness. He still maintained a sense of humor in his last hours. Joe and I stayed all night. Terry made it through the night and into the next night. He passed away in the middle of the next night. We had gone home to rest a bit in a fitful sleep.

We knew his departure was coming soon and felt if too many people were around, he wouldn't go. Joe fell asleep beside me late at night. I couldn't wind down. Suddenly, like with Adam, I felt it. I knew he was gone. I must have said something aloud because Joe stirred and said, "What?" I told him we needed to be prepared for a call. Just then the phone rang. It was Becky. I said, "I know he died. I felt it." We left right away. Ryan was a basket case, and it was all we could do to soothe him.

On January 12, 2019, we celebrated Terry's life. We drove through a snowstorm. Nothing would keep us from Terry. Like with Adam, cardinals flooded our porch and yard, a pretty good sign they had met. The service was beautiful. Mac and Joe sang, "Go Rest High on that Mountain", by Vince Gill, while Joe played the guitar, and Mac played his harmonica. Terry had wanted that, although we didn't know if either of them could do it. It was beautiful. Terry brought a lot of people to God in such a short time. He will be remembered by all of LifeQuest. Lil' Man said, "Nana, church will never be the same." And it isn't, but we all carry on just like we do after our other losses. We meet new people who we have to set that example to, to love on, and to give hope to. Thank you, Terry Luna, Papa Terry, Big T. We love you! June 9, 1957-January 6, 2019. Fly high!

Joe and I didn't quite know what to think. We had lost so many people in so few years: both sets of parents, our son, our beloved Aunt Jane, and now Terry. So many others had lost family to suicide, including great friends, Clay and Annette, Robbin and Jerry, Krissy and Mike. One thing we can certainly say is, we are not alone.

On February 22, Joe turned sixty years old! We had a few friends over from the VFW and church. Stephanie and Marlon Sr. came. Marlon had everyone cracking up with his stories. It gave me joy to see how much he lights up Stephanie, how he is the bright spot in her life. She was giggling along with the rest of us. I stood next to her and put my arm around her. I knew how difficult it was for her to show up with her anxiety issues. I said, "That wasn't so bad, now was it?" She told me that it was. I had no idea. She put on a brave front just for her dad. She cherishes him so much. How unfair that she has to live with so much pain and suffering. Like with Adam, I would gladly trade places with her so she could live a happy life.

March came. Joe and I had been married thirty years before on Adam's birthday. He would have been twenty-eight. It was our third birthday/anniversary without him.

During March, we took the cruise that Terry Luna had planned. Joe and I renewed our wedding vows. Becky officiated in Terry's place. He told her he wanted that. We missed his physical presence so much, but we knew he and Adam were there in spirit. Joe and I both read personal vows with our friends, Becky Luna, Krissy Revert, Dave and April Morgan, and Shawn and Sue Teagarden surrounding us. Mac stood by Joe and Kristina stood by me as she had done thirty years before. We could both barely get our words out. We cried like babies. Through that experience, we realized how blessed we truly are with our love for each other, the love of family, and of treasured friends.

On the first Friday of April, we had a NAMI event in conjunction with Save One Life with Mike and Mindy Horton, whom I have had the honor of getting to know very well over the last three years. We often help each other's group out as we deal primarily with mental illness and they deal with recovery from addiction, yet both often go hand in hand. I had met a lady named Anna Cole, who has a beautiful venue in the West Bottoms of Kansas City in a large old brick building. She holds many weddings there. She is passionate about NAMI as she has two siblings with mental illness. She let us use her space. We called it "Sing Out the Stigma," a karaoke with dinner catered by Olive Garden.

Some of us shared experiences and others sang. It was a fun night. Dear friends from church came, along with neighborhood friends, John and Mylissa, and some of our karaoke group, including Bill and Cindy Wilmurth (Bill ran the karaoke equipment for us), Bill and Mary Fort, Jim and Sharon Parcel, and Susan Sanders. Mac and Kristina, ever faithful, helped us out, and of course, we got to enjoy Mac and Joe and the gang singing!

During April, Missouri NAMI's Executive Director, Gena Terlizzi, was pushing Joe and me to go the annual state conference in Jefferson City. We had not yet had the pleasure of meeting her in person, so we agreed. We also knew that Elizabeth Wilson, my treasured friend, wanted to go but had no way to get there. Joe got her a room at the hotel, and I sent her a message, letting her know she would be accompanying us! She was as giddy as a kid. I loved it! We had an enjoyable time. The three of us, along with Bentley, traveled to Columbia, dropped him off with Mac and Kristina, and then headed onward.

Elizabeth was the most delightful companion, and true to form, she took pictures for us as we had been nominated into the NAMI Hall of Fame! We couldn't believe it! No wonder Gena wanted us there!

Following that, we stayed the next night with Mac and Kristina. We took Elizabeth to church at cousin Gary Powell's Revolution Church. She did amazingly well. I felt so proud to call her my friend. We headed home that afternoon, dropped her off in North Kansas City, and made our way home.

Joe went to the men's retreat with LifeQuest that month, and Marlon went with him. The people who went wondered where we had hidden him all this time. It was life changing, and he loved the experience.

In May, I went to my second women's retreat and spent my first birthday without Joe in thirty-one years. The plan was to go to Krissy Revert's dad's place out in the country in Warsaw, Missouri, with her, Kelly Zaloudek, and Robbin Loftin. We got some sun and went fishing the first day and then headed to the retreat the next day in Clinton. Sadly, Krissy's dad had a heart attack, and she spent that time with her step-mom, Elaine, and Kelly at the hospital while Robbin and I looked after their pets, a dog, a cat, and a bird! It rained all day, so there was no sun and no fishing.

Robbin and I took a tour of the place, as she had family there and knew the territory well. We had a nice day and met up with the others for dinner at a local Mexican restaurant, where the waiter put whipped cream all over my face! Didn't expect that!

The retreat was a lot of fun, and the ladies bonded even more than ever. We were divided into teams. Each team had their own bandanna color. Ours was dark purple. This was fitting for me, as purple is the color for suicide prevention. My good friend Mindy Horton was in our group, along with Jamie Smith from the worship team, another dear friend, Chrissy Prescott, and a lady I wanted to get to know better anyway, Tina Leonard's (from worship team) mom, Mary.

Mary did massages by appointment from her cabin. I received one of these. While she was massaging my back, she stopped suddenly. I learned later that she was very prophetic. She looked right at me and told me that I was not done. "Do you understand what I am saying? You are so not done." I didn't know exactly what that meant, but she motivated me to keep on going and trying hard to reach out to others. She gave me that last push that I needed to finish my story.

I had time off during the summer for the first time ever in my life, and I had two major goals. One was to recover from my illness (I had discovered the answers the day before the women's retreat) and to finish my story. I hoped and prayed that I could accomplish both as Joe and I had a travel-filled month of June.

We kicked off travel in June with an airshow and camp out with NAMI friends and advocates, Marty Sexton and Trisha Wear. Her son Ben is stationed at Whiteman Air Force base near Warrensburg, Missouri. He joined us.

Following the airshow, we returned to Kansas City for one day. Pastor Chris has a vision that gets me excited. I had attempted to incorporate my desire to bring mental health awareness in the churches and schools with our previous walk in 2018, with LifeQuest being one of two to get involved. Chris has more connections than we do, and he got a group of pastors together for a luncheon. It took place at Keller Williams in Overland Park, Kansas (Pinion Realty), with Angelique Daut, whose daughter is an apprentice at our church. The purpose of the luncheon was to ignite interest in a future conference (spring of 2020) to bring mental health awareness into other churches like we have done in our own, to put NAMI groups into place, and have an outreach program.

So many pastors I have spoken to have told me one of the greatest needs in the church is to help families with mental illness. As we know, that is one in four people, so you can bet it affects the people in your church! Some of the diagnoses are extreme and others mild, yet it affects one in four.

My cousin, Pastor Gary Powell, attended, as did my friends

pastors Jim and Sharon Parcel from karaoke. It was too short but got the point across. We were praying for great success for the following spring!

Unfortunately, that was canceled due to the COVID pandemic. Pastor Chris still has hopes it will happen in the future when life gets back to "normal".

Joe and I went to St. Louis the next day, clear across the state to join his brother Steve and his wife Connie to see Carrie Underwood in concert. From there we drove back across the state, through Kansas and into Colorado. Our next event was a wedding near Denver, but we had friends near Durango in the mountains of Bayfield that we wanted to visit, too.

It was Glen and Susie Green from Oklahoma, the ones who had lost their son to suicide on Christmas Day 2012, the day Adam slipped away the second time. Susie was the one who was there for us day after day but never revealed their loss so we wouldn't give up hope on Adam's recovery. She is a jewel. Our sons, Bryce and Adam, were close friends growing up.

Glen opened up about the loss of his son, Blaine, something he rarely would do, except for Susie, but he knew we understood the loss. During the day, Susie worked and we bonded again with Glen, just in a different way. We have known each other for many years now. Our children had brought us together in the beginning, and now we were bonded in another way, belonging to the club no parent wants to be a part of, the parents of a child lost to suicide.

We said a tearful good-bye as we left for Denver. Still, we were excited to make it to Denver, too. One of my kids from my first years in child care was getting married! We attended her big sister's wedding in September 2015 in Texas where they live. Spencer, the oldest, is due to have her first child this September, and Schyler is now married, too! Their parents, Craig and Leslie, have been dear friends since the early days of Broken Arrow, Oklahoma, and though we live far away, we all make attempts to reconnect whenever we can. A destination wedding is a great excuse!

We had a wonderful time and had a little time to catch up. It ended way too soon, but from there Joe and I headed to Colorado Springs for a few days to ourselves before heading back to Kansas City. We hiked a lot during our vacation and packed a cooler so I could eat foods I am not allergic to. We went to the top of Pike's Peak (by car), walked on the Seven Trails, and visited Garden of the Gods. We ate one night out there at a German restaurant called Edelweiss. It reminded me of my travel to Germany as a youth and Papa's cooking at home. They had a gluten free menu, and it actually tasted authentic, too! I was in heaven!

We made it home and headed into July. I only participated in the fireworks tent at LifeQuest on the fourth of July (the busiest day) for a couple of hours. I intended to stay longer but had an allergic reaction to Off spray so I had to leave. "Grandma" Deana and J.R. Flemming from church ran the tent this year since Terry had passed away. It was well organized and fireworks sold out. Joe spent much of the week there. I worked on *Adam's Contract with God* and completed it that week! Then I began writing this book.

Now for months we had been praying for Kristina to get a job in Kansas City, as she and Mac grew closer. We didn't want to lose him to Columbia, and she was now a part of LifeQuest, too. She had been living in Mom's house since her divorce and after Mom's death but knew it was only a matter of time before Medicare would take over the house to pay for Mom's nursing home expenses.

As it happened, the courts decided it would be taken August 12. Kristina had been interviewing for months and sending out job applications. She was accepted at UMKC to begin July 23, and all of her benefits, retirement and otherwise, transferred from UMC in Columbia! She recently moved. For the first time in our married lives since our move to Tulsa in 1989, we have family living here! Answered prayers!

During July, Mike Revert presented me with a beautiful granite box he had created for Adam's ashes. They had been in the original container from the funeral home since he died. He made one for Joe and me that match, and we plan on being interned with him when we pass away. I returned to my full-time job as a nanny in August for my last year.

In September, for reasons we will never understand, after all the love and support we showed to Lil' Man over the previous years, he decided to leave all of us and live with his mother in Colorado.

We closed out 2019 with Christmas with brother Martin's family. We are now the orphans, so we get to go to various family members' houses during the holidays. We are so thankful for all the love of both the Custins and the Shultzes.

Chapter 16
2020 Vision

In January 2020, I felt renewed. I had finally published *Adam's Contract with God*, and it felt like a weight had been lifted off my shoulders. I finally felt ready to face the world. It was scary because I literally bared my soul in that story. I had a vision that this was going to be the best year since Adam died. I had many events lined up for the coming months—events that many people had worked hard preparing for.

The first one was to come in March, my book signing, along with a fundraiser for NAMI and SAVE ONE LIFE (founders Mike and Mindy Horton) with dinner and karaoke. Our dear friend, Bill Fort, was our karaoke man. Our VFW friend, Susan Sanders, bought a box of my books for the book signing. My friend Lorna came from Louisiana with her daughter Jacy and her son Kayne from Tulsa. My sisters, Ann and Kristina, were with me, and Krissy Revert, Kristina, Mac, and Joe had helped our team prepare during the previous months with Mike and Mindy. Michael Brown donated lots of artwork and got to sign the book, as he is the artist on the cover. It was a success in spite of COVID! No one got sick due to the event. Other VFW friends attended, including our dear friends, Ron and Julie Johnson, and Jim Nail.

The next event was the Missouri Annual C.I.T. convention in Columbia, and Joe and I were invited as speakers!

Then came the NAMI of Greater Kansas City walk, the first one that would happen since the reinstating of NAMI in our city, which happened in April.

Lastly, we attended a conference on mental health for pastors around our great city, which our pastor, Chris Pinion, started with great passion. I couldn't run support groups for families with NAMI, but some people emailed me or messaged me to update how they and their loved ones are faring.

Spring break came for the family I nanny to in mid-March. COVID-19 hit in 2020, and schools closed down for the remainder of the year. I did go back to work after a couple of weeks to care for the kids part time while their mom and dad got some work done at home.

Sadly, all of our events were canceled. We still had hopes of having some of them in the fall, but the quarantine lasted longer than expected. By June 2020, some things were gradually opening up, but with social distancing (keeping six feet apart and wearing face masks in public). In my 2020 vision I had never envisioned that!

As in many cases, some good can come out of bad things. Joe retired from State Farm at the end of February, so we were able to spend a lot of quality time together. He worked hard on the project of finishing our basement and doing some remodeling on the main floor so we can enjoy our music, friends, and family at home.

Stephanie came around a lot because she needed to use our printer for a little gig she had going, and the library was closed so she had to come here. She is seeking support online for her trauma and told me she is ready to live again!

In June 2020, we were hoping and praying to be able to have our event, Sing Out the Stigma, in September, a karaoke, a dinner, a book signing, and fundraisers for NAMI and SAVE ONE LIFE. Many people were so kind about the first one being canceled. My sister, Kristina was on the committee for the event, and she told me that she was most disappointed because I had worked so hard to reach this milestone. This was very sweet, but like I told her, "It will happen, just in God's time. Not mine."

Well, it did happen in September of 2020! We wore masks and sanitized the microphones, and no one got sick from that event. My sister Ann came from St. Louis, and a friend, Lorna Hesskamp, flew in from Louisiana! Kristina and Mac were there, along with my planning committee, Krissy Revert and Joe from NAMI, and our Save One Life team, Mike and Mindy Horton. It was a success!

Mac proposed to Kristina in 2020, and they made plans to marry in June 2021!

All in all, 2020 shaped up to have some good visions ahead!

Chapter 17
2021

In December 2020, a woman named Robin Walsh requested me as a Facebook friend. I accepted, as we shared two mutual friends. A woman I don't even know approached Robin with a copy of my book, *Adam's Contract With God*, and told her she NEEDED to read it because Adam's story aligned closely with her own.

Robin is the author of *My Morning Song, Psalms 23: My Journey back from Suicide*. We met for coffee in January 2021 at 9 a.m. I didn't make it home until 2:45 p.m. She is the reason I wasn't to complete this story the year before! I was supposed to meet her first. The bond we have forged is incredible and is as if we have known each other our entire lives. We were born only a year apart.

The next time we met, the following week, I got home close to 5 p.m.! We meet together as often as possible. She has started a nonprofit organization called Choose To Live. It is about saving lives from suicide. We have plans for future suicide/mental health awareness events, and I can't wait to see what the future brings for both of us through this sister-like bond we share!

On June 6, 2021, she held a golf tournament recognizing people who, although attempting suicide in their past, ended up making great contributions to the world. She also honored the lives of those who had died by suicide, our son being one of them. As Robin puts it, she is the voice for those who can no longer speak. Krissy Revert came with me for support. Joe formed a team with Jacob Kalianov, Matt Edmonds, and Blake Cavalier. All had a great—although emotional—time.

In 2021, C.I.T. trainings increased in the rural counties, and Kansas City began in-person trainings once again.

In March, Joe and I were honored guest speakers for the Annual Conference, which included all of Missouri. We have now been requested to speak further out into the different areas of the state. It is our favorite "gig" for raising mental health awareness, and it so rewarding witnessing lives being changed. My hope for the near future is to continue with that, along with events like "Sing Out the Stigma" and putting together events that NAMI, Save One Life, and Choose2Live can all be a part of, incorporating all the things that affect our mental health and sharing ways to cope, saving more people from suicide and the abuse of mind-altering substances.

Later in the year, with the help of many others (including my kiddos, Nick and Sadie Peterson, who helped rip out old floors and assist in other ways, Mike and Mikey Revert, Mac McDonald, Ariel Haney, Mikey's best friends, Morgan and Sammy, Mike Kovaleski and his son Dustin, and of course, Joe) remodeled our upstairs (I painted!) and finished the basement. Our basement is no longer a cold reminder that Adam chose to die in a concrete slab with concrete walls. It is now a place of comfort and beauty, something Adam would love.

For Adam's would-be thirtieth birthday, we had a karaoke in that place. We celebrated his life in a fun and loving way and dedicated the space to him and his life. With God in our lives leading the way, I see positive changes in our future. We know we will still have our bad days, as everyone does. At the same time, we know that there is healing, love, and comfort all around us.

Chapter 18
Resources

This chapter covers some resources you can look into for help with struggling to cope with a mental illness or as a survivor of suicide. Personally, one of the best support systems I have found is the "Families Dealing with Suicide, The Next Chapter", an amazing support group which people from all over the world join. You certainly do not feel alone there, and even though you might find yourself overwhelmed at first by the numbers, you will discover so much love and acceptance and a free zone to speak any time of your loved one. Someone is always listening and reaching out, and you even discover new friendships along the way.

- Suicide Fighters Support Group (Facebook) is more for those who have made suicide attempts and are struggling to navigate this world and survive it!
- MOS, Mothers of Suicide (Facebook).
- Save One Life (Facebook). Administrators and founders Mike and Mindy Horton offer support to those overcoming addiction. SOL is a Christ-centered group, but you will feel no judgment. As we know, addiction often goes hand in hand with Mental Illness.
- Out of the Darkness Walks to bring awareness to suicide and prevention of. Go to afsp.org/outofthedarkness to find a walk in your area.
- If you live in Missouri or Kansas, check out one of my favorites, SASS-MO-KAN, Suicide Awareness Survivor Support, to find a live group in your area. SASS provides walks for awareness and

healing days throughout the year.

- Choose 2 Live, a non-profit dedicated to bringing hope to those struggling with mental illness, depression, suicide, and self-injury. http://www.choose2live.org/
- You can also reach Robin Walsh, executive director at my4s1s@ yahoo.com
- National Suicide Hotline: 1-800-273-8255 or text 741741
- The National Alliance on Mental Illness (NAMI). If you are a family member of someone with lived experience (a person living with a mental illness), I strongly encourage you to take the Family to Family course. Please, if you are a family member or someone living with mental illness, find a support group near you. You will be glad you did. And never stop advocating for yourself or your loved one. You are making a difference one person at a time!

Chapter 19
For the Love of Adam

This chapter is dedicated to the people who loved Adam during this life. These are stories, tributes, or comments individuals shared with me. Some are happy; some are sad, but all reflect life with its ups and downs.

Adam was kind, compassionate, quirky, funny, lovable, and most of all, he loved God and knew where he was headed. I hope you can feel how Adam's love permeated every soul he encountered in this life.

Ann Shultz, my sister shared: *Remember that time I came to your house in Broken Arrow to help you after one of your surgeries? Adam came out of the bathroom to show me his penis. (This was before we knew he had Schizophrenia.) He was totally naked. Funny thing is, I thought it was normal.*

Ann, thank you for the time you spent with my children over the years. One thing Joe and I talk about when we think of memories of our past, is that it isn't the things we had or received that we remembered. It was the time that was given to us. You gave that to our children even when we couldn't go with you. Our children received the gift of adventure with you as you traveled around the country the way we used to do when we were kids. I am forever grateful. Both Stephanie and Adam spoke fondly of these times over the years. How fitting was it that Adam's last trip was planned and carried out with you as our leader? God bless you for your time, Ann! I am also thankful to you for the "vacation" time you took for the coma in 2012, the death of Adam in 2015, my NAMI walks, and your regular phone conversations with Adam. He really loved you. Thank you for recognizing how important that is to me. I love you! Thank you for holding me up when we removed Adam from life support.

Debbie wrote me her memories of the days at St. Joseph Hospital: *I will never forget the first words that Adam said to me when he came back to us. Everyone had left to go grab something to eat, and just the nurse and I were with Adam. I was brushing his teeth with one of those sponges and he said, "Ah, minty fresh." I asked the nurse if she heard him say that, too and she said, "Yes, with his eyes as big as saucers.*

Boot mugs and red balloons will always be special to me. (Boot mugs from a plastic boot mug Adam had on a Custin family trip to Branson. He kept singing in his Okie accent, "I got my boot mug". We were all laughing, and he fell down and broke it. He was so sad. His sister gave him hers.) [Debbie's little girl was the one Adam saw in heaven with a red balloon.] *And to this day I remember him every time I put on Chapstick. I guess I am a lip Nazi* [her name at St. Joseph for constantly putting Chapstick on his lips]. *Adam gave me the greatest gift a mother could ask for: knowing that her child was in heaven.*

Debbie, thank you for all the time you took off work to help us out during that time, after Adam's death, and with the NAMI events. Thank you for all the text messages and the first Christmas without Adam. We love you very much!

Little brother, Martin, thank you for always holding my heart. I love your tenderness and care. Thank you for taking the time and being with us during the most difficult days of our lives. Thank you for loving us and our kids the way you do. Thank you for your sense of humor, too. Thank you for treating Adam like a man and making him feel like he belonged. Thanks for taking his calls and talking to him when he needed it, even when he was in psychosis. I love you so!

From Martin: *Thinking about the time he came out of the coma at St. Joseph Hospital. He kept showing his penis to everyone who came in the room; family, nurses, anyone! We couldn't keep him covered! He kept insisting he needed a strawberry flavored Shasta, and well, he just got out of a coma and I left and searched everywhere and couldn't find it. I brought back a different flavor, and he denied even asking for it in the first place. He also told me when he "woke up" that I looked so more Mexican than usual.*

Ahh. That's my quirky Adam!

My brother, Jimmy and Suzanne, thank you for getting us away to take time to think about life as it is now. Nature was what we needed at that time. Suzanne, thank you for staying with us during the coma and beyond. Thank you for loving Adam "for who he was", as he put it. He loved you guys and initially wanted to be a tree trimmer when he "woke up" because of Uncle Jimmy. Jimmy wanted to share how much it meant to him that he was the one that Adam first spoke to when he woke up from his coma in 2012 after everyone believed he would die.

He said: *I came through with my son Austin and some other guys from work on our way to a job in South Dakota to pay my respects, and he woke up and spoke to me!*

Suzanne goes on to say she wasn't actually in the room the night we removed Adam from life support because she felt that was going to kill him. She felt and knew he would survive it! She said she meant no disrespect, but it was how she felt. God Bless her, she was right!

Kristina, how does one say thank you for three-and-a-half years of listening to us cry and living real life with us? Your support has meant the world to us, and there is nothing we could do to possibly thank you. Simply being in our home during weekends and getting us out into the world has made such a difference in our recovery. Also, thank you for being there during the coma and following. I will never forget, "Go to the light, Adam!" when you thought he took his last breath and then he woke up the next day! I am so happy you are now in Kansas City forever, and so happy you found love again with Mac.

Kristina writes: *When Adam was born on March 4, 1991, he was a beautiful boy with bright blue eyes and blond hair. Throughout his childhood, he could win anyone over with his mischievous grin. He was always quite the character and loved to joke around. He was "normal" to anyone who knew or met him.*

One of my daughters, Jessica, was only a year older than him and less than five months younger than his sister, Stephanie. They spent many of their holidays and spring breaks together, along with their other cousins since they lived six hours apart.

I say "normal" as that is something everyone has said in their life, myself included. What is "normal" though? According to the dictionary, it is conforming to the standard: usual, typical or standard. So are any of us "normal" all the time? No! When Adam was probably around 14, some of his jokes became concerning at times. He was being his quirky self, but some things as outsiders were questionable. Was this "normal" boy stuff or teen stuff? It's hard to put a timeline on things since we were not together all the time, so I may be off on his age.

They lived in Broken Arrow, Oklahoma, and we lived in Columbia, Missouri. As one of his mom's sisters, I was always a phone call away. I remember Heidi calling me with various "Adam Incidents", ER visits, near-death scares, etc. Some that stick out are him inhaling compressed air from a computer air duster, taking Stephanie's insulin and syringe (he was caught before using), stepping out in front of a car, overdosing on morphine pills, and last his final attempt in which he completed suicide at the age of 24 on Christmas morning when he hanged himself. I began working in the disability field in 2005 at the University of Missouri-Columbia. I worked in the School of Health Professions for ten years before moving on to Student Affairs in 2015. When I entered the disability field, I learned very quickly how wrong I was, along with so many others, about people who suffer from a mental illness or any disability. Some of the myths are that anyone with a mental illness is crazy, violent, or dangerous, has mood swings, or PTSD, or that if they would just stay on their medications, they would be okay. Wow, were all of those wrong!

As many parents do, I compared my two children and two step children to other children who had issues in school, disciplinary problems, or poor behavioral incidents. Unfortunately, there isn't a guide to perfect parenting, and we all learn as we go, and every child is different.

When Adam first started having signs of Schizophrenia, none of us knew, including his physicians and parents, but as I look back on his early stages and signs, I was just as guilty as the next person by judging him and his actions. I thought that if he would get a job as a teenager, worked more hours, played sports, had a better choice of friends, or was disciplined more, he would change his behavior and actions. My children started working at the age of 14, part time after school, weekends, and/or during the summer. It kept them busy and taught them to appreciate working for an income.

I also had each of them involved in at least one activity or sport each year. While this kept them busy and gave them spending money, I still don't know if it was the right thing to do, but it worked at the time. Behind my sister and brother-in-law's backs, I would get so frustrated for them, thinking Adam was just fighting for their attention. At one point, I was even supportive when they talked about sending him to a boy's camp as that would straighten him out. I would encourage them to ground him, be stricter with him, take things away from him, etc. What I didn't know was when they did these things, nothing changed his actions. He was ill. Very ill. And none of us knew what he was going through until the last few years of his life.

In November 2012, Adam overdosed on morphine pills. He was declared brain dead, and my sister and her husband made the difficult decision to take him off life support. What none of us knew was that we would witness a miracle when he spoke four days later as we took turns sitting beside his bed, waiting for him to die. After a long recovery and physical therapy, Adam came back to us in a different way than he had been the previous eight years. He used the next two-and-a-half years to educate us on Schizophrenia and mental illness. He gave us hope. He showed us love and expressed it to his friends and family.

Sadly, the voices came back, and he succumbed to his illness and died Christmas morning in 2015. Did he change Christmas Day for all of us in one way or another? Yes, of course, he did. We will never forget that morning. However, my sister and brother-in-law and niece's lives have been changed forever.

Initially, my thoughts were that Christmas will never be the same, and later I felt selfish as I saw how Heidi, Joe, and Stephanie have had to wake up every day knowing that Adam is never going to come walking through his bedroom. Sadly, I felt a sense of relief, and I knew he was not suffering and no longer in pain. I understood why he completed suicide. I knew I wouldn't or couldn't live like that.

During our years of Adam's recovery and not having the voices driving him nearly insane every day, he had told us if the voices came back, he would complete suicide the next time, which he did. When Heidi asked if I would write how Adam affected me and my life or how I truly felt during those ten years of highs and lows, I immediately agreed. I tried to summarize it briefly, but it is impossible to do so. What I can say is it is easy to judge a person, a situation, a family or friend, but if you are not walking in their shoes, you have no right to judge. I was just as guilty as everyone out there. For that, I apologize. I learned a lot while working in the disability field, but I learned a whole lot more witnessing my nephew's life. I miss Adam, his quirky jokes, his genuine love, and his beautiful smile. I am so glad that he is a peace and no longer in pain. Keep watching over us, Adam! Your story is educating so many others and for that I am thankful because a part of you lives on. I love you. Until we meet again...love, Aunt Kristina

Megan Elise Rainey wrote this to me February 2016, so keep in mind she has been on an uphill climb ever since. She is an amazing young lady who struggled like Adam and loved him fiercely. She stuck by his side all his years since she met him, even long distance in KC. She shows up at NAMI walks and visited him a few times during his recovery and has been a great support to me since his passing. I love you so much, Megan!

She wrote: *I first met Adam in ceramics class in the ninth grade. Around this time, I was pretty much the uncool kid that could never do anything outside of school. I'm not exactly sure how we became friends. We just rode the same bus and lived in the same neighborhood. He meant a lot to me from day one. I had a pool in that neighborhood, and I remember him picking me up and throwing me in. Ha ha. After that a year or so later, I was able to sneak around to be with my friends.*

Adam was already part of that group. There were so many memories there. One that comes to mind is when he was trying to get into the car with someone and ended up falling out and taking a good chunk out of his chin. Not sure what happened after that. Me and him got a lot closer this past year. I loved his laugh, his goofiness, his carefree loving attitude. He was one of the most open-minded people I've ever met. I remember when I went to Disney World one year with my dad and sisters, and I was probably on the phone with him 80% of the time. One night I even stayed up all night sitting on the bathroom floor talking on the phone long distance. All night. Lol. He loved his friends. He loved talking and knowing how everyone else was doing to the day. A lot of our convos lately was him asking, "How's so and so?", always asking about everyone and how their lives were going. I would say, "I'm not sure, Adam," but would fill him in on what I knew. He seemed different to me in a good way (post coma) and judgment-free when it came to anything.

Toward the end when I would visit him in KC, I could see some changes occur. He could hear whispers and felt someone was talking badly about him. I tried to tell him it wasn't true. He truly believed it was, though, and there was nothing I could do about it. One night at the hotel, Adam and I sat outside and talked for hours. It soon got very heavy. He talked of his depression. I had no idea how bad it was. All the telephone calls were cheerful, and he hid all that very well. He was very lonely in his head. He cried talking about all this. I had never seen that before. While he was talking, I did my best coming up with the right things to say, but you know me. I'm not so great with words, so I was making a flower out of my cig butt, and when he was done, I handed it to him. He went from crying to laughing and crying. He thought that was the coolest thing ever.

When I was leaving Kansas City, I finally let him hold me like a baby. He was trying to do that the whole trip, and I wouldn't let him. Lol. I cried leaving that driveway because he told me us coming saved him. I didn't want to leave. When hearing about 2012, I thought I'd already lost him. It broke my heart just like it did this time. However, when I found out he was pulling through...well, I can't describe that happiness. It was the best day ever when me and Cary were able to surprise him on his birthday at the rehab hospital. Adam's miracle affected me in so many ways. After I saw that video, I showed it to everyone. Back then my faith was already pretty strong. But this last year it wasn't so much. But his story at one point was the ONLY reason I still hung onto God.

I was having a really bad night about seven months ago. I myself did not want to go on, and I had lost all faith in my higher power. When I told Adam about it, he told me, "Well maybe you should get yourself into a coma, haha." He told me not to worry because God is real and Heaven is a real place.

After his coma, I never lost touch with him again. Especially, all of 2015. He was always there. I always thought I needed him more than he needed me. I talked to him a lot almost every day up until the Tuesday before he passed (he died that Friday). Most of the time, it was all good stuff. Some of the time we were both really struggling, but no matter what, Adam was DETERMINED to make me talk and help me. He was there when I felt completely alone a lot of the time. He was hilarious all of the time. He would tell me to stop laughing because he wasn't funny, and I would say, "YES, you are!" And then he'd be like, "Yeah you're right, I am funny." in that excited high pitched sarcastic voice. Haha.

Before the voices started coming back, he talked about school.

He really wanted a car. I wrote a funny poem once about his dream for a car. That dude loved the heat. Always talked about how he couldn't wait to mow the yard in 100-degree weather. Lol. He mentioned going to school to write.

As far as the voices returning, yes, I could tell. Most of the time he was bothered by the whispering. He never understood WHAT the whispering was actually saying. One of the last times I talked to him, I was coming home from the gym. I missed his call while I was there, and when I called back, he was panicking. He was so relieved to hear that I was okay because he thought he accidentally sent a demon to get me. I asked him if he was okay, and he said, "Well, yeah, I am now. Well, Megan, I got to go." I never wanted him to feel like he wasn't okay, so I never questioned him about those off things...maybe I should have.

Adam's death affected me a lot. I already lost multiple other close people, and this one was just unbearable. I soon felt a peace, though. I saw him and was with him (though it was long distance) til the end, and I know he is finally where he wants to be. Back with God. I'm sober three months today [now it has been over three years] and stronger than ever. I talked with Adam at my all-time worst, and when I decided to turn my life around, he was always calling congratulating me. Telling me things like, "Hey at least you remember last night."

Always little things to keep me going. Things I will never forget. He is still alive in my heart, and I will think of him every time I hit another milestone in my sobriety. He is an enormous reason why I have made it as far as I have and how far I will go. Adam helped change my views and open my eyes. I will cherish his loyalty and friendship forever. I made sure to tell him I loved him every single time before we got off the phone. I've learned that life is truly precious, and you have to tell people you love them because tomorrow is never promised. That was just a saying to me for so long, but I'm glad I learned the truth of it before I lost him. I know he knew I loved him. I can't wait to see him again.

Thank you, Heidi, for always being so kind to me. Thank you for being supportive and thank you, thank you, thank you for bringing Adam into this world. He meant so much to us all.

The same month Megan sent me that, her sister, Kara wrote to tell her she had a dream about Adam:

I saw him smiling and his mom was happy because she said he was doing better now and that he was really happy. I wasn't going to tell you because that's really sad, but it's also nice because I felt that maybe he is in a good place now and he is happy all the time.

She added: *My family loved him. Who couldn't?!*

Megan and I still keep in touch and lift each other up long distance. I feel connected to her because she was such a huge part of Adam.

A year ago, Megan wrote this and sent it to me:

Maybe I do not even need to write about it.

Maybe I can just let it be.

But it must be known how amazing it is to be…in love with yourself and with who chooses to be with you the same.

How beautiful it is that we are alive at all?

That we cry and we fall but always recall

the courage to stand up again.

It is only with love of a friend we need.

In the darkest moments we plead to be freed.

We want a purpose though it's not hard to lead.

I read and read about self-healing.

Like it's some hard thing to keep breathing.

Have you ever been on the ground begging for a break?

Knowing what was at stake...

you feel minutes away from the end

but it's just prayers you choose to send to mend

what has been broken...

To be forgiven for what you have chosen.

Have you been cold and alone

begging to be shown

what is possible if anything

maybe a being that cares

when nothing seems fair.

And now you're here.

Looking in the mirror.

It's been you all along singing your own song.

You feel like you've been found,

but it's your God that has been crowned.

You have never been without

and that's what life is all about.

Love will always find you.

You cannot find this yourself.

It is not a book on a shelf.

There is no secret to love's wealth.

On Earth you may feel alone

because you are not yet back home.

But home one day we will all be

and you will surely see

that everything that we have wanted to be will create the word...ME.

December 25, 2018, Revelations 21: "He will wipe every tear from their eyes. There will be no more death or mourning or crying or pain, for the order of things has passed away."

June 5, 2019, *Hey, Heidi! I wanted to share a dream I had last night. I was in a gym for an assembly at some school. I was sitting on the ground with a bunch of people but didn't know anyone. I then heard Adam's voice and turned around, and he was joking with some teacher...being Adam. And before he turned around and saw me, I said, "Hey buddy." He immediately turned around, and we intensely hugged for a long time, and I kept hearing the teacher say, "Okay, okay that's enough. Break it up." And we did after a couple of more seconds and both said, "It was so good to see you." And I woke up. It's been on my mind all day, and I don't have those dreams often enough and thought you'd want to hear about it. Hope all is well.*

Jamie Lynn Smith, a waitress we saw frequently at a Bob Evans in Belton, Missouri, before it got shut down shares: *I don't know if this will help you or make you cry or even both, but I want you to know the impact your son had on me. When Bob Evans shut down, I started a new serving job three days later. I was getting yelled at by the cooks and treated poorly because it was my first day, and I was not trained in that store. I didn't know the menu, and the guests in Kansas are vicious. I began to feel so worthless. So useless like how did I have five years of experience? How was I so bad at this? I had to remind myself that with every job, you have to take the time to learn. I couldn't just walk in and run the place at Bob's. Well, a guest told me I had the worst service they had ever seen. He said it's amazing I could even pass as a normal functioning human in society, and that they shouldn't hire servers that are challenged. I began to get angry. I sent a manager out to finish the table.*

I went outside, and just as those words were starting to sink into my head, I thought about you, Joe, and Adam. I didn't know that I helped Adam until you told me. [Jamie treated Adam like everyone else, not like someone with a disability. She joked back and forth with him and had a huge impact on him.] *But it made me remember that I am not any of those things. That even if I could make one person smile in a day, that would be enough to make my job not so pointless. You never know what people are going through, and in your son's tragedy he helped me. Every time I get down, I think about the smile you brought to me when I had an exceptionally difficult night. You guys are so sweet, and I am so grateful that we were able to help each other. Adam was so sweet and such a lil' cutie. You guys were always so nice to me. I want to thank you for that. You guys deserve the world, and one day Adam will be with you again. You are just not finished helping servers like me and so many more yet.*

Our neighbor, Christian, born the same year and month as Adam, got to know him when we moved to Grandview in 2012 and spent many hours and walks/talks with Adam. He traveled with us in 2013 to Memphis during Adam's recovery. He is a very bright young man who had infinite patience with Adam. Thank you, Christian!

From Christian following Adam's death: *I am glad I got to take that trip with your family to hang out with you guys and Adam. I'm glad that while he was here I got to enjoy his friendship. He was an amazing guy.*

From our very dear friend of twenty-seven years in Oklahoma, Traci Foster: *I have two memories that keep jumping in my brain, shouting "Pick me, pick me!" So here we go. Both Adam and Alex went to St. Benedict's Mother's Day Out program in Broken Arrow. I believe it was the three-year-old class. Every day Alex would come home telling me stories about his new best friend named Adam. He couldn't wait to go to preschool to see his best friend, because, well playing with his baby sister wasn't any fun.*

One evening we were standing outside in the front yard and Alex starts yelling, "Adam!!" Next, I hear a kid yelling, "Alex!" Then Alex starts running down the street and runs into the arms of—lo and behold—his best friend, Adam! It was like a love scene out of a movie. That evening we met your family, learned that you lived four houses down the street, and the lifelong friendship began.

My next memory is when the boys were in first grade and we received phone calls from the principal's office of Andersen Elementary. It seemed as though someone had dared Adam and Alex to pee outside during recess. Our boys took that dare, tee-hee, and were trotted off to the principal's office. I do believe after that scenario, Adam and Alex no longer had classes together. I have to say that remembering back to the days that the kids were growing up, we had the best neighborhood and group of kids. Adam, Alex, Carson, Nathan, Bryce, John, Max, Stephanie, and Shelby all had a great time playing and running around the neighborhood. I couldn't have asked for a more fun group of kids and parents to have been blessed with in my life. I miss seeing everyone!

Love you, Traci Foster

From our beloved neighbors, Tim and Lorrie Gordon: *How does one pay tribute to someone that was only in their life for such a short time, yet left a permanent mark on their heart? We met Adam in April 2013 when we moved in next door to his parents. Adam had recently been released from the hospital after a long recovery from yet another suicide attempt. We came to learn Adam's story from his parents and neighbors. Instantly, we could see the miracle that he was.*

As the months went by, we were so happy to see him grow stronger and more alert. Some neighborhood families would gather once in a while for dinner out, jam sessions at the Custins' house, or just stand around outside to talk. By that fall, Adam was doing quite well with his relearned motor skills and was very outgoing. A group of us spent the day in Independence for the SantaCaliGon Festival and lunch on the Square.

A memory that always makes us chuckle to ourselves is that while we walked around the festival, Adam would come and go. But he always returned with yet another treat. We're not sure how many he got or what they were exactly, but we all knew we were going to be lunching soon, so it was kind of comical to us. Adam was just like a kid with a pocket full of money in a candy store!

Adam, we miss you as a friend and neighbor. We feel extremely blessed to have known you. Thank you for teaching us through your childlike innocence how to be more patient and accepting.

From my friend, Lorna: *ADAM, I am truly blessed to have met such a sweet, caring person. I met Heidi in Early Childhood classes in Broken Arrow, Oklahoma. We hit if off right away and our friendship grew. I met Adam in her home when he was only nine months old! I can still picture him sitting on the floor with his mom and I. He was a happy baby!!! My next memory was when he was eighteen months old doing puzzles for older children, 24-36 pieces! What a smart little man!!*

With Heidi and I having our own in childcare/preschool, we would put our heads together and attend many functions together. We would also take our children on field trips together. Heidi inspired me to grow as a person. We would amaze adults on our field trips with the good behavior of so many children together! We could take the kids out to eat pizza and never have an issue. Heidi could take her kids to my house for educational events, or meet at parks for play dates.

When Stephanie and Adam were small, they sure could get into mischief! I can still hear Joe giving them the talk! Heidi and I would stand around the corner listening and giggle sometimes. Adam would later tell us those talks were pretty funny and oh how his dad could talk!!

I had a daughter only a few months younger than Stephanie. They were friends and had a lot of get-togethers through Girl Scouts. It was hard having sleep overs. Both girls were very active in other areas and attended different school districts. Adam became close to my daughters. My older daughter thought of him as a younger brother. Adam and Stephanie were very close to each other. Stephanie dragged Adam along with her to the park with her friends. She loved her brother and it showed.

In 1998, my marriage began to fail. Heidi and Joe would both be there to support me, love me, and guide me. It was a very difficult time being homeless. Here is where the beginning of my relationship with Adam grew, along with my trust. During 2001, I had to move from Oklahoma to Louisiana. One of the hardest things I ever did! The first year was hard; it seemed like I had lost all my friends in Oklahoma with little communication at first, with no job, which meant no phone.

In 2002, things began to change; I got a job and a phone and a place to live, and I got my daughters settled. That's when Heidi and I reconnected. Then a trip back to Oklahoma (2006) and Adam was so excited he let me sleep in his room. I remember him telling me about his wall decorations. I do believe one of them came from Hooters!! He had no shame! But then we had a unique connection and respect and love. Heidi and I began long weekly talks. We were sisters designed by God's love.

I have to stop here and reflect on how blessed I am to be a part of the Custin and Shultz families!! I met both sides of the family. Heidi's mom only briefly. I do believe she visited once and I happened to stop by. I remember when Stephanie and Adam's cousins, Chris, Tad, Will, Brittney, and Jessica would come for a week or so during the summers and meeting Heidi and Joe's brothers and sisters, as well. I remember praying for Will when he was born too soon at less than a pound, so tiny! I could not wait to meet that little nugget! I got to meet Joe's side of the family during a wedding close to where I live, where I ended up filming the event, Joe's mom and dad, sister Debbie, brother Steve and their kids, Jimmy, Sam, Sarabeth, Abby, and Alesha. I am richly loved.

In 2005, my oldest graduated from high school. Kristina planned a friends and family cruise. So for a graduation gift, we went on the cruise. I know my daughters were happy to reconnect and spend time with Adam and Stephanie, as well as Jessica. All I know is the kids were inseparable and had a wonderful time. They were also honest with us. The girls went skinny dipping right in front of us! Adam let the girls bury him in the sand and create boobs on him and other things with the sand while he lay there taking it all in! Little did we know, he was drinking on the beach and he was only fourteen! This was the beginning year of the turmoil Adam would go through the rest of his life.

On one of my trips to Oklahoma, I got to stay with Adam so Heidi and Joe could go on a much-needed visit with family. Adam and I went on a dinner date. We both looked forward to going. I let him pick the place and the time he wanted to go.

During dinner, he talked about his aspirations, his future, and what he wanted to do with it. School is what he wanted at the time. He said he wanted to go to California and work in the film industry, not acting though. Oh, I wish I could remember what it was called! We talked about Scouts and growing up. He said all he could remember was my friendship with his parents. Then he thanked me. "For what?" I asked. "For being you!" he said. It was an amazing night for both of us. I felt like the voices left him alone for the first time in a while.

The rest of the week he did not lock himself in his room. He actually would come out and watch TV with me, and sometimes he just wanted to talk. We had popcorn night, pizza night, and fend for yourself night. I was blessed that week.

My memory is not great from here on out. I do remember being with Heidi on the phone during each event with Adam and I can't go into detail of these events. Why? Because each time I would pray that Jesus would use me to talk to Heidi. I know He did! I can remember the calmness that came over her. You will read about these if you read Adam's Contract With God.

Heidi and I continue a close relationship, talking weekly on the phone, filling each other in on family and events. We have laughed and cried, used each other's shoulders, and lifted each other up. We talk about our jobs, have goofy laughs and good cries. We both have lost family, friends, and even children we have cared for. The joys Adam brought to the family outweigh the troubles he went through.

I am a follower of Jesus. The last conversation I had with Adam was about his visit to heaven during his near-death experience. I confirmed to him it was real and there was a reason he came back and was doing so well. He said he came back for his sister, Stephanie! He wanted her to believe, too, and know that Heaven is for real! For three years since Adam passed, a cardinal has perched on my fence looking at me through my dining room window. I told him it's okay. I am good now. Jesus has me. Then it hit me! Adam was thanking me for being there for his mom! I said, "You are welcome! Remember she is there for me, too!" That was the last time I saw the cardinal.

Thank you, Adam, for that extra warmth I needed when I slept in your bed that cold October night. Thank you, Heidi and Joe, for such a fabulous friendship! Thank you is not enough. May God bless you and keep you and restore you anew.

From Betsy Adams, a young lady Adam became close to during his last year or so. She lived in Tulsa, and they had met briefly a few years before. She was one of the people who talked with him for hours when he needed a friend. She and Adam had a long-distance romance for a while.

Betsy says: *Adam and I would talk every day. I worked at Burger King as an assistant manager at the time. I would put him on speaker phone while I was counting money and such. We would talk for hours. I loved talking to him. He could make me laugh so much. He got my humor. He knew my problems. I felt like I could have talked to him about anything. We wanted to be together. I was falling hard for him. He always made me feel so confident about myself. We always played Words With Friends, and even though he never admitted it, I know he would let me win because I was so bad at it. He had the best laugh, so contagious. I loved hearing it. Adam called me the day before he was gone, Christmas Eve. I was driving to work, running late so I told him I would call him later. Then I got busy at work and never called. I found out the next day what happened. I was crushed. My heart broke that day. I feel so guilty for not calling him back. In my head, I could have prevented what happened. I still think about him constantly. I miss him so much.*

I replied: *Dear Betsy, you could not have prevented his suicide any more than we could have. He was hurting and in so much pain none of us could possibly comprehend. I am certain he called to talk to you one last time because you meant so much to him. I love you so much for being there in ways we couldn't during the last months of his life.*

From my beautiful NAMI friend, Felice McDaniel: [We had a board meeting at our house one time.] *I can see Adam in the kitchen when I was at your home and he called me "the girl with the curly hair". He will always be a precious gift.* [Adam was in high psychosis that day and felt fearful of a group of people in our house. Felice is in her 70s, and he had never met her before. He was drawn to her from across the room. Her hair is much like mine. Maybe it was that or just the kindness that exudes from this lady.]

From another NAMI friend and current board member, Carol McGraw: *I haven't really stopped thinking about you two since I read Adam's Contract With God. What a beautiful gift he was to the world, and Heidi, it was a gift to get to know him through your book.* [Carol lost her son Jason, who also lived with Schizophrenia, from congestive heart failure due to medication he took for his illness.]

From another author in Colorado. Matt lives with Schizophrenia and belongs to a group of advocates called the Schizophrenic Alliance Group. He contributed in writing, "Crazy: An amazing mental health resource". "Crazy" is an award-winning art book created by youth for youth as a visual "insider's guide" to what depression and anxiety feel like and how they can affect your daily life and relationships. One-hundred-fifty artists between the ages of 15 and 25 contributed. Most were in high school, college or working. It is incredible!

January 27, 2020: *I finished your book tonight and brought it to my Schizophrenics Alliance meeting. I am so sad to hear about Adam's passing, and I felt so down for a while, which is okay by me, because I learned so much from him in the book. You are such a strong and active person, and I feel you did everything you could to keep him here with us. I would love to hear more about your story and am looking forward to your next book! I passed the book on to my mom. She is reading it now. Thank you so much for being brave and sharing/opening up your-self so others like me do not feel alone.*

From Tess Fekas, our amazing ICU nurse when Adam was in his coma in 2012: *When does life begin? At conception? Birth? A child's first step or word? When they graduate high school and start "college life" without the "parents in tow"? When does life end? When the person can no longer speak, hear, or care for themselves? When a person tries to take their own life? When a person is on life-saving measures in the ICU, or when you withdraw those life-saving measures? When they become an organ donor? Or does life end when their heart stops and a part of your heart stops, too?*

The Bible tells us that God can change impossible situations. He sometimes moves mysteriously, but will provide what you need in miraculous ways. And it is going to be far better than you can ever imagine. So, do what you can and God will successfully execute what you can't. Ecclesiastes 3: 1-8 tells us, "For everything there is a season, a time for every activity under Heaven. A time to be born and a time to die. A time to plant and a time to harvest. A time to kill and a time to heal."

Nurses can see these seasons; I am that ICU nurse. What happens when you witness the first breath of life and last breath of death? What happens? Sometimes miracles happen. This is how Adam and his family came to me. The critical, fragile young life came to me by Adam's own hand. He had attempted to end his own life, and now, iron-ically, was on life-saving measures. Adam's family were familiar with his struggle of the "voices" due to Schizophrenia and his mental illness state. However, this struggle would be in uncharted territory for this family and like no other previous struggle.

Adam came to the ICU from the floor due to his deteriorating state and his MRI status. He was now unresponsive and was diagnosed with acute encephalopathy. Adam was now also on sedation, a venti-lator, feeding tube, and several IV bags hung by his bedside. He was brought to the ICU due to needing a higher level of care due to organ failure, being on life support, and because medicine is there to help, heal, and to provide hope, right?

Heidi and Joe, Adam's parents and I, began to know one anoth-er well. Adam's sister, Stephanie was by his bedside, as well. Heidi, Joe and I would often speak about not only Adam's course of care, but we would also speak of how our faith was prominent in our lives. We did a lot of talking, hand holding, and crying. I would also talk to Adam each morning as I would wash his face and hands, despite his unrespon-siveness, and tell him what was happening each day and how much his family loved him.

It was Christmas season, and sometimes I would sing a Christ-mas song to him as I was caring for him throughout the day. Then I would laugh and tell him that I couldn't wait until he woke up and told me how bad of a singer I was! I always maintained hope.

However, as the minutes turned into hours and hours turned into days, many physicians had come and gone without Adam's status changing. I had taken Adam for several neurological scans, and the scans did not reveal a good outcome. Adam's story now laid in the neu-rologist's hands. After the neurologist and I spoke, I called the family in so that we could all sit down for a meeting regarding Adam's outcome.

As the multitude of the family members sat in the conference room, the neurologist explained that Adam displayed no brain activity, the ventilator was breathing for him, his organs were continuing to fail, and that the next step would be withdrawal of care. Unfortunately, there was nothing more to be done. As everyone wept, the neurologist explained that withdrawal of care is when you remove the ventilator from the patient, cease all life support measures, and allow the patient to pass on with comfort measures in place. I then addressed the family and explained what they were about to witness through tear-filled eyes. I was crying so hard for this family and the loss of this young life. After all, I had a daughter not much older than Adam, and a mother's heart strings are strong for their children. I could not imagine this heart-wrenching scenario. Heidi would say that she would stare at Adam and try to memorize his face, so she would not forget one single detail.

During this season, we were to be awaiting the Christ child's birth, not the death of this child. As I looked at the family, it took everything for me to say, "Let's give Adam a Heavenly Christmas with God our Father. He would tend to Adam." I also explained that once I removed the life-saving measures that were in place, that I would leave them all together as a family.

As we returned to Adam's room, Heidi, Joe, and Stephanie had decided that they wanted a small intimate service before I removed his life support and asked if I would stay. I was humbled as I made the arrangements, and the neurologist and I prayed with Heidi and Joe. I gave the family three red hearts to signify the Father, Son, and Holy Spirit that would be taking care of Adam. What else can you say or do for a family that is about to lose their child? Stephanie said that she would keep them for her brother. That afternoon, as the hospital priest spoke, we all stood hand in hand around Adam's bed, our tear-filled eyes and heads bowed, as Heidi and Joe played a beautiful song entitled "He's My Son". Adam's life had seemed to end; did he accomplish his goal? Did he make the "voices" stop? Or did only one voice remain? God's voice. The final say.

When an ICU patient has been withdrawn from care, they pass at various times, depending upon the disease state. However, Adam did not pass, despite all of the neurological scans nor the neurologist's expert observation. His heart continued, as did his breathing, despite not being on the ventilator. When this happens, the patient is moved to a room on the medical floor so that the family can have more privacy during such a difficult time.

After my shift was over that night, I visited Adam and his family on the floor to say goodbye and wish them peace during this Holy season. As I entered the room, they were all placed around Adam's bed. Joe had brought up his guitar and they were all singing at the bedside. They stated that he was unbelievably holding his own.

A couple of days after Adam had been moved, another ICU nurse excitedly ran to me and asked if I had heard about Adam. I was confused regarding her excitement. She stated that Adam had opened his eyes. I was sure she was inaccurate. I was caring for critical patients at the time, so I could not go see the family. Not soon after I learned this information, Adam's neurologist visited me and confirmed the news, Adam had opened his eyes! We both cried. And as he was apprising me of Adam's progress, he hugged me and stated, how lucky are we, that God chose us to be a part of a miracle and to show us his Majesty! I was stunned and speechless. How could a patient with no brain activity open his eyes and then utter a word? Despite medicine, highly trained doctors and nurses, sophisticated testing, despite it all, God was in control. It truly was a miracle.

In the following months, Adam continued to improve. He had to learn how to talk again, how to move, and how to walk again. He was weak, had pressure ulcers, and struggled, but still progressed. I was amazed at the daily news of his small accomplishments. When I went to see him, he did not remember me; he was weak, his body still reeling from the stresses it endured, but he could stand with a walker and smile! Also, the "voices" were gone. Yet another miracle! The torment Adam and his family had endured for years was gone.

As the weeks and months flew by, Adam progressed through his physical, occupational, and speech therapy, and his body continued to slowly heal. Adam, with his family by his side, persevered. Just uttering his name or his parents' names was progress. Although there was progression, Adam would falter and have to begin again. It was not an easy feat. After some of his physical therapy sessions, Heidi and Adam would come and visit me at the hospital and show how far he had come and what he could do or say. I would continue to be amazed. Although time would show me that at this point, what amazement was.

After a long duration of therapy at rehab, Adam's physical healing was complete. How wonderful that his body healed. He could speak. He could function daily, and the "voices" remained far away. But there was one more miracle on the way. Heidi called to inform me that Adam was going to begin classes at a local college! Yes, the mental capacity was there! They seemed to have their Adam back. All of the smiles and I love you's were back. Adam had planted his feet firmly, took those oh so small steps, and arrived here. He was on his way to harvesting all those strenuous days he lived through. The family even began to take small trips together again. No one would know the struggles or triumphs this family had seen through their smiles in their photos as they captured one more day with Adam.

However, after a trip in the summer to Montana, Heidi sadly reported that the "voices" had returned. The struggle, fear, and pain of Schizophrenia was back. Remember those seasons? Remember Ecclesiastes 3: 1-8... "For everything there is a season, a time for every ac-

tivity under Heaven. A time to be born and a time to die. A time to plant and a time to harvest. A time to kill and a time to heal." Remember the struggles and triumphs during these long years. Another was on its way again.

Three years earlier, I had stood before this family with tears in my eyes and stated, "Let's give Adam a Heavenly Christmas with God our Father. He would tend to Adam." Three years later, Adam would take those words that he never heard me utter to heart and took his life on Christmas Day while his family was at a relative's home. The voices were gone. Adam was gone. As I learned of this tragedy, my heart sank for this family a second time.

Medicine teaches you pathology, physiologies, disease states, and medical principles. But it does not teach you about the intertwining of lives. Some people and events will leave indelible marks in your life. You learn that life is fleeting and precious. You learn to cherish every word spoken and every smile you see as you pin them to your heart. You remember Heidi's words as she said that she would stare at Adam and try to memorize his face so she would not forget one single detail. Yes, that. Do that. Every day.

As I entered the funeral home and looked at Adam in his casket, he looked just as he did in that ICU bed. Only this time there would be no ventilators, no therapies, only wings.

I opened up this book with my daughter Stephanie's story. This is Joe's story saved for last, as it is only fitting. Joe is my amazing husband, the greatest dad and husband that ever lived in my book, no matter what he says! I love you, Joe!

Adam's death was shocking and bitter. He was my son and he is dead. Did he do it for himself, or, maybe, for everyone else; to prove his suffering was real? I simply don't know and, frankly, why does it matter? I'm left with no wisdom, no intelligence, and nothing to offer but tragedy. My thoughts are figurative since replaying his life in my mind brings extraordinary discomfort generated from my own failure and ineptitude. Nothing about the way we found him hanging from a floor joist in our basement brings feelings of accomplishment or success. The real culmination to death was from years of distress, mistrust, frustration, anger, fatigue, disbelief, and accumulated crises of epic proportions. Adam's sad journey was a free fall to the next lower plateau, and I will always be left wondering about my own attitude, own motivation, and my own will to help him. Was it enough?

The questions during his illness always haunted me. Get tough, don't be so tough, get on medication, get off medication, ignore the problem, don't ignore the problem, let it go and give up, don't let go, be supportive, be calm, be enraged, confront other people, other kids, teachers, school administrators, doctors, don't confront them, give greater responsibility, remove responsibility, force school and work, back off school and work, kick him out of the house, let him stay, let finances destabilize over tragedy, be more frugal, inform family of crisis, keep crisis secret. As each serious crisis arose, I always felt we were "over the hump" and Adam would "snap out of it." We could be a "normal" family with a few "bumps and bruises" and lead him to a productive, stabilized adulthood.

It was not to be so. My solutions, good or bad, to piles of problems simply didn't work. Relentless frustrations, always. The truth is the truth. Adam died and I didn't save him. I felt like Heidi gave me more credit than I deserved in handling family issues. I somehow thought that modeling the right behavior would be the solution. In other words, do a I do, not as I say. That was the primary reason for being involved in their lives through leadership in sports and scouts. I wanted to show my children my willingness to work hard, accomplish education, wor-ship God, volunteer in community, have great family relationships, have great fun, enjoy excellent friendships, and, most of all, be a person of good standing. On the other hand, I was consumed with career and the prospects of greater monetary reward.

I honestly believe that as a young man, my priorities were wrong, being consumed with making money. I was always thinking about impending problems and opportunities, and I believe it crowded out clear thinking and proper attention to the problems of my children. Instead of researching financial markets, business psychology, leader-ship, problem resolutions, and studies, I feel I should have done more research in helping my children.

I always felt like other parents had clever solutions to handling kid problems where I drew a blank. I reasoned that being my best would translate into organically healthy children. I believe Heidi and I were a great team. I'm grateful for her. I felt she was more in tune with Adam and took his problems more seriously than I did. I thought we were dealing with a phase that would go away. Of course, it never did. Hei-di was different. She had a sense that things were terribly wrong. She helped mobilize my thinking from finance into the right direction where it counted, and we were able to realize Adam's incredible miracle be-fore his death. We really did realize the most incredible awakening from tragedy and spent two-and-a-half amazing years with Adam as a nor-mal young man.

As Heidi says, "We got to meet the young man Adam was sup-posed to be": good looking with great humor, high energy and joy. Every day was amazing during that time. We generally cooperated with one another during times of discussion and we never, ever blamed the other for the immense problems we faced. We looked for paths we felt

*were doable, not impossible feats, but things we were capable of ac-
complishing, like who will take Adam to work, how are we going to
get him to the doctor, how can we find the money for college? We both
used the talents or resources we had individually to solve community
problems.*

*I believe Adam felt secure living in our house knowing that we
had ways to solve problems. I'm happy to have known Adam. His illness was extremely frustrating, time consuming, and expensive. Schizophrenia can be an ugly, ugly disease. He desperately worked to protect
us from his own despair. He truly cared for us and was gentle with us
as his own frustration would allow. He loved animals and nature and
because he understood pain, he felt deep compassion for the world. I
don't blame him for taking his life. In many ways it was not a choice,
but a consequence of a serious disease.*

*He was a great man. Adam taught me a lot about life and death.
He died, and yet, somehow, he was/still is with me. I wanted to know
about his whereabouts, and through the miraculous power of Christ
Jesus, I am energized to push out with what I know and help others.
Adam talked of Heaven the first time he died and being in the presence
of God. Adam's words on Heaven were of beauty and love. And it reminded me of his life.*

*I pray I was the best father I could be. I love my son as I love my
family. My way to see him will be to cross over in God's presence. How
amazing will that be?!*

Epilogue

I feel an overwhelming sense of love and gratitude, yes JOY at the completion of something I never thought I could possibly accomplish in my life. There are so many people who made this possible for me from life before and with Adam to those who came into my life afterwards. So many people to thank for the support and love you have given me.

Thank you, all my LifeQuest family! You know who you are!

Thank you to each and every person I have ever encountered through NAMI. How I ever made it until I met you, I will never know! Thank you to my family, especially Joe's, and my siblings and nieces and nephews! You light up my world.

A big thank you also goes to the cover artist, Gary Powell, my first cousin on my father's side of the family. We grew up very closely together. Gary was a huge player in Adam's life, as not only a family member, but as clergy. He is the pastor at The Church of the Revolution in Columbia, Missouri, where he resides with his wife, Audra. He helped Adam navigate the waters of life and death, Heaven and Earth. He is also owner of Ernie's Signs & Banners. He and his church prayed for the miracle of 2012 when Adam returned from brain death.

Special thanks to my husband Joe, who walks this journey with me every day of my life. Your love, kindness, patience, and support through the dark days, as well as times of joy, mean so much to me! I cannot imagine a world without Joe Custin in it! You make such a difference in so many people's lives, including my own. I never really lived until I met you. I love you!

Special thanks to my daughter, Stephanie, and her unfailing love. I am so blessed to be your mom. I cannot thank you enough for living this journey with me. I would be lost without you! I love you! Special thanks to my illustrators, Michael Brown, (front cover of *Adam's Contract With God*), to Pastor, artist and cousin, Gary Powell (for the front cover of *Living the Legacy of Adam*). Thank you to my editor, Leanna Brunner, for your faith in me and your unending patience.

Most of all, I give thanks to God for always being with me in joy and sorrow, to guide me through this journey, and give me strength to find the answers I need to survive. My prayer is that I have helped make Adam's legacy something he would be proud of me for. He had such an impact on my life. Writing both stories was a long, arduous task, filled with a lot of tears and laughs, too. I told someone a while back that this was taking me so long to finish. She said it was because my story continues, and it will keep going. I want you to know that your story isn't over yet either.

I joined the Semi Colon Project some years back while Adam was still living. Sadly, and ultimately, the founder took her life but made an impact on so many lives. The semi colon means the sentence hasn't been completed; the story hasn't ended. The project was intended to give suicide survivors hope (those who had attempted and lived) that their story continues. I took it a step further in my story of my son. I realized that my own story, his too, has not ended. It goes on, and yours will too, if you speak up and advocate for your loved one or speak of the one you lost. Make his/her life count, make a statement, and advocate because like me, your story has just begun. Look for the signs. Our loved ones who passed are still with us, and I believe with every cardinal or heart or dream I see and feel, Adam is with me saying, "Go on, Mom! Keep living! Keep fighting until we eradicate mental illness from this earth! Don't hold guilt and shame. It is a waste of your time and energy. Go in peace and love." I will continue to fight for my son, Adam's legacy! How will you live your legacy?

9 781087 985190